Health and Human Development
Units 3 & 4

First published in 2024
Insight Publications Pty Ltd
3/350 Charman Road
Cheltenham Victoria 3192
Australia
Tel: +61 3 8571 4950
Email: books@insightpublications.com.au

www.insightpublications.com.au

Insight VCE Revision Questions: Health and Human Development Units 3 & 4

ISBN: 9781923154964

Written and reviewed by Katherine Jones and Natalie Burke
Cover by Melisa Paredes
Edited by Julia Carlomagno
Internal design and layout by Bec Yule @ Red Chilli Design
Printed by Markono Print Media Pte Ltd

Note: Some articles were written in previous years and so may include some dated references.

Insight Publications acknowledges the Traditional Custodians of the Country on which we meet and work, the Boonwurrung People of the Kulin Nation. We pay our respects to their Elders past and present, and extend that respect to all Aboriginal and Torres Strait Islander peoples.

Contents

Introduction iv

Questions 1

Unit 3, Area of Study 1: Understanding health and wellbeing 1

Unit 3, Area of Study 2: Promoting health in Australia 12

Unit 4, Area of Study 1: Global health and human development 35

Unit 4, Area of Study 2: Health and the Sustainable Development Goals 48

Sample responses 59

Unit 3, Area of Study 1: Understanding health and wellbeing 60

Unit 3, Area of Study 2: Promoting health in Australia 73

Unit 4, Area of Study 1: Global health and human development 93

Unit 4, Area of Study 2: Health and the Sustainable Development Goals 105

Introduction

Insight's *VCE Revision Questions: Health and Human Development Units 3 & 4* contains questions, suggested responses and tips to develop skills for assessment, including the end-of-year examination. The questions cover all the areas of study in Units 3 and 4 of VCE Health and Human Development. A good habit to try to implement is to test yourself by working through this resource. The process of actively recalling information assists with deeper learning, and it helps that you can check whether your answer is correct.

By using this resource as part of your study regime throughout the year, you will be prepared for questions you may encounter in your VCE exam.

We wish you well with your studies.

The Insight Team

Questions

Unit 3 | Area of Study 1 Understanding health and wellbeing

Question 1 (10 marks)

a. Describe spiritual health and wellbeing. 2 marks

b. Using an example, explain the relationships between the dimensions of health and wellbeing. 5 marks

c. Outline one way in which optimal health and wellbeing can act as a resource at each of the following levels. 3 marks

Individual

National

Global

Question 2 (4 marks)

Smoking: Quit program	The Quit program has worked hard to phase out tobacco advertising on television and radio. It has also encouraged changes to laws regarding plain packaging and non-smoking areas, and has a Quitline that offers support and advice for those trying to give up smoking.
Skin cancer: SunSmart program	The SunSmart program encourages schools to have policies such as 'no hat, no play' and advocates for shade when planning outdoor spaces. SunSmart also has an app that informs people of the UV levels for the day and a catchy slogan, 'slip, slop, slap, seek and slide', which encourages people to slip on a shirt, slop on some sunscreen, slap on a hat, seek shade and slide on sunglasses.
Road safety: Driver Reviver program	The Driver Reviver program opens up to 220 Driver Reviver sites across Australia each holiday season. These are located along popular routes and offer places for drivers to stop and refresh, with free tea, coffee, snacks and toilet facilities. The Driver Reviver program involves volunteers from the State Emergency Service (SES), Country Fire Authority (CFA) and Lions Club. It also has tips online for driving safely.

Explain how **one** of the programs above could lead to optimal health and wellbeing as a resource, individually and nationally.

Question 3 (7 marks)

a. What is meant by 'life expectancy'? 1 mark

b. In Australia, women generally experience a longer life expectancy than men.

Using one environmental factor and one biological factor, explain the differences in life expectancy for men and women. 4 marks

Environmental factor

Biological factor

c. The gap between male and female life expectancy in Australia is projected to decrease.

Using **one** sociocultural factor, explain why this may be the case. 2 marks

Question 4 (4 marks)

a. Explain the emotional dimension of health and wellbeing. 2 marks

b. Using an example, explain how a person can have poor emotional health and wellbeing, yet still experience good overall health and wellbeing. 2 marks

Question 5 (3 marks)

In 2012–2013, the proportion of Aboriginal and Torres Strait Islander peoples aged 18 years and over who did not meet the daily recommended intake for fruit and vegetables (two serves of fruit and five serves of vegetables) was 97%. In comparison, the national average was 94%.

Explain how this could impact the health status of Aboriginal and Torres Strait Islander peoples.

Question 6 (6 marks)

a. What is meant by 'burden of disease'? 2 marks

b. Outline the difference between YLD and YLL. 2 marks

c. Identify a disease or condition that may result in higher YLD than YLL and justify your response. 2 marks

Question 7 (5 marks)

The following graph shows the number of deaths for different geographical areas.

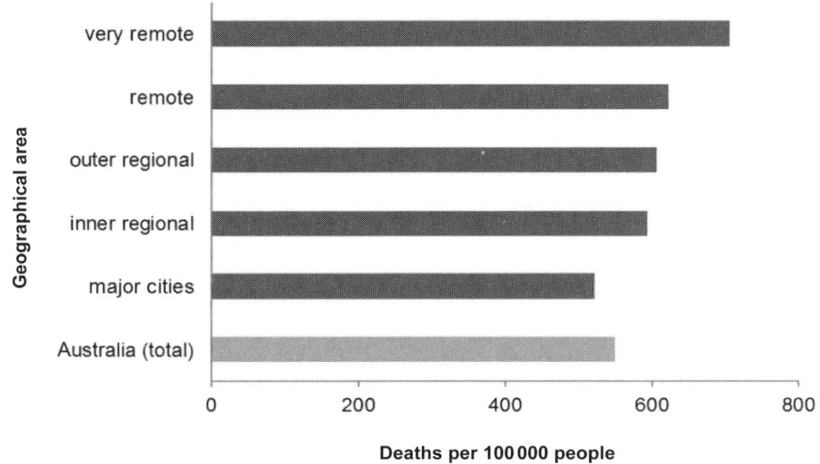

Source: Australian Institute of Health and Welfare (AIWH), <https://www.aihw.gov.au/reports/rural-health/rural-remote-health/contents/deaths-remoteness>; licensed under Creative Commons Attribution 4.0 International, <https://creativecommons.org/licenses/by/4.0/legalcode.en>

a. Outline the relationship between geographical area and number of deaths shown in the graph above. 1 mark

b. Select one sociocultural factor and one environmental factor and explain how each could account for the relationship described in **part a.** 4 marks

Sociocultural factor

Environmental factor

Question 8 (4 marks)

Explain the social and physical dimensions of health and wellbeing.

Social health and wellbeing

Physical health and wellbeing

Question 9 (2 marks)

Explain how mental health and wellbeing is a global resource.

Question 10 (4 marks)

Figure 5.5: Life expectancy at age 65 in full health (HALE) and ill health, men and women, by remoteness area, 2015

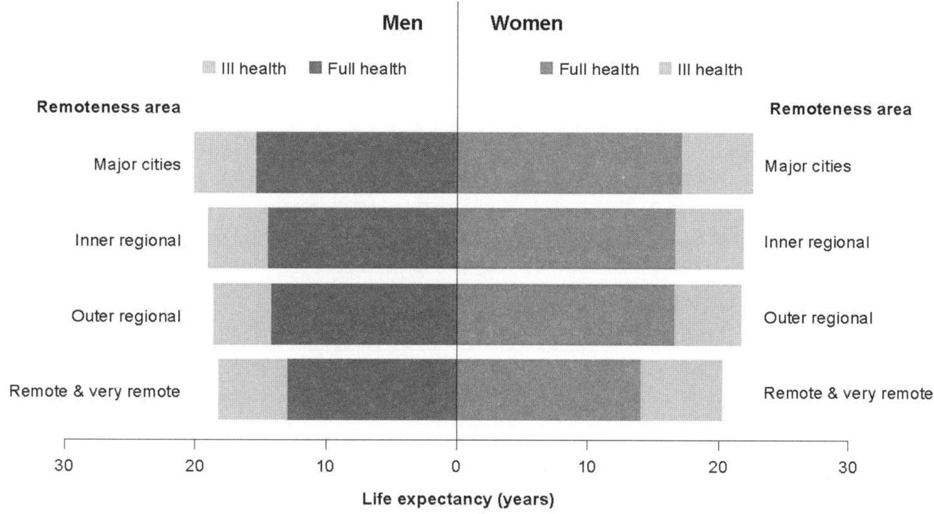

Source: Australian Institute of Health and Welfare (AIHW), 'Australian Burden of Disease Study: Impact and Causes of Illness and Disease in Australia 2015', p. 55, <www.aihw.gov.au/getmedia/c076f42f-61ea-4348-9c0a-d996353e838f/aihw-bod-22.pdf.aspx?inline=true>; licensed under Creative Commons Attribution 3.0 Australia, <https://creativecommons.org/licenses/by/3.0/au/legalcode.en>

a. Describe health-adjusted life expectancy (HALE) as a measure of health status. 2 marks

b. Using the information from the graph, outline how remoteness impacts on the full health (HALE) and overall life expectancy of men and women. 2 marks

Question 11 (6 marks)

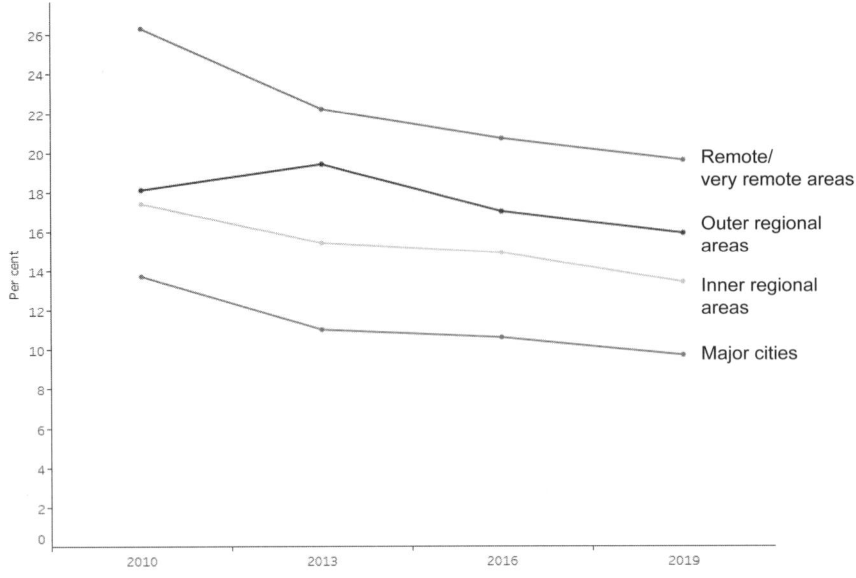

Source: Australian Institute of Health and Welfare (AIHW), 'Alcohol, Tobacco and Other Drugs in Australia', Figure TOBACCO 3, 2024, <https://www.aihw.gov.au/reports/alcohol/alcohol-tobacco-other-drugs-australia/contents/drug-types#atriskgroups>, accessed 19 March 2023; licensed under Creative Commons Attribution 4.0 International, <https://creativecommons.org/licenses/by/4.0/legalcode.en>

a. Identify **two** trends in the graph. 2 marks

b. Using data, explain how smoking could contribute to variations in health status between the population groups in the graph. 4 marks

Question 12 (3 marks)

Victorian Workplace Mental Wellbeing Collaboration

VicHealth, SuperFriend and WorkSafe Victoria have formed a collaboration to help workplaces create positive and supportive cultures and environments that enable workers to be more engaged, positive and effective at work.

Victorian workers spend around one third of their time in the workplace and the work environment can provide a positive sense of community and connection with others, as well as build self-esteem and provide recognition and rewards for individual workers and teams.

The engagement with workplaces will focus on providing information, resources, and tools on positive mental wellbeing interventions such as developing a positive leadership style, designing jobs for positive mental wellbeing, communicating effectively, recruitment and selection of employees, work-life demands, and supporting and developing employees.

Source: Adapted from Living Well Vic, 2018, <http://leadingwellvic.com.au/about/>

Explain how the Victorian Workplace Mental Wellbeing Collaboration is addressing health and wellbeing as a resource nationally.

Question 1 (2 marks)

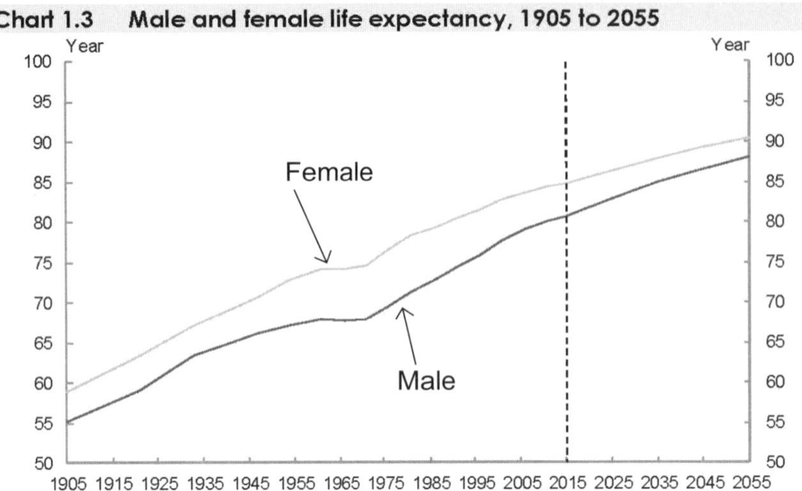

Source: The Commonwealth of Australia, 2015 Intergenerational Report: Australia in 2055, chart 1.3, based on ABS cat. no. 3105.0.65.001 and Treasury projections, <https://treasury.gov.au/publication/2015-igr>; licensed under Creative Commons Attribution 3.0 Australia, <https://creativecommons.org/licenses/by/3.0/au/legalcode>

Using the information from the graph above, draw a conclusion about the impact of the social model of health on life expectancy.

Question 2 (2 marks)

In 2012–2013, the proportion of Aboriginal and Torres Strait Islander peoples aged 18 years and over who did not meet the daily recommended intake for fruit and vegetables (two serves of fruit and five serves of vegetables) was 97%. In comparison, the national average was 94%.

Many food models recommend a high intake of fruit and vegetables. Many Aboriginal and Torres Strait Islander peoples have been exposed to such food models.

Explain **one** strength of food models, such as the Aboriginal and Torres Strait Islander Guide to Healthy Eating, in changing the dietary habits of Aboriginal and Torres Strait Islander peoples.

Question 3 (6 marks)

The Australian Government funds and oversees many initiatives aimed at educating Australians about dietary choices.

Using your understanding of dietary change and the challenges faced by organisations that focus on dietary change in Australia, evaluate the capacity of **two** Australian Government initiatives to influence change.

Question 4 (6 marks)

The following graph shows the number of deaths for different geographical areas.

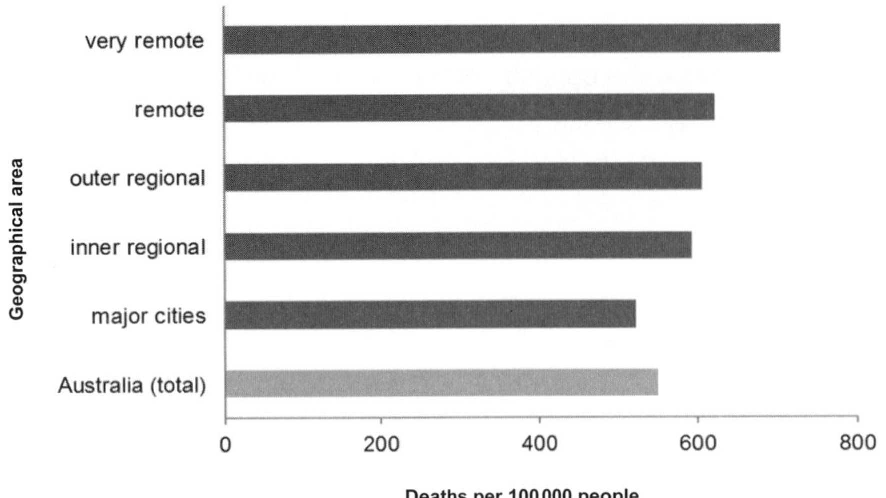

Source: Australian Institute of Health and Welfare (AIHW), <https://www.aihw.gov.au/reports/rural-health/rural-remote-health/contents/deaths-remoteness>; licensed under Creative Commons Attribution 4.0 International, <https://creativecommons.org/licenses/by/4.0/legalcode.en>

Identify two action areas of the Ottawa Charter for Health Promotion and explain how they could be used to decrease the differences displayed in the graph above.

Action area 1 ______________________________

Action area 2 ______________________________

Question 5 (4 marks)

a. Describe private health insurance. 1 mark

b. The Australian Government wants more people who can afford private health insurance to take it out.

Explain why the Australian Government wants more people to take out private health insurance, and include **one** way the government encourages Australians to do this. 3 marks

Question 6 (7 marks)

a. Briefly describe **one** health promotion program that has been developed to improve population health. 3 marks

b. Explain how the program described in **part a.** reflects **two** action areas of the Ottawa Charter for Health Promotion. 4 marks

Question 7 (6 marks)

The Australian Government funds Medicare, the Pharmaceutical Benefits Scheme and the National Disability Insurance Scheme (NDIS).

a. Describe Medicare and explain how it can improve the physical health and wellbeing of Australians. 2 marks

b. Describe the Pharmaceutical Benefits Scheme and explain how it can improve the health status of Australians. 2 marks

c. Describe the NDIS and explain how it can improve the emotional health and wellbeing of Australians. 2 marks

Question 8 (4 marks)

The Yarning it Up – Don't Smoke it Up tobacco project, provided by the East Metropolitan Community and Population Health Service, aims to reduce tobacco-related harm in the adult Aboriginal population of the Perth metropolitan area of Western Australia.

The project delivers workplace information sessions to service providers, focusing on the Yarning it Up – Don't Smoke it Up project, stages of change, the journey to quit tobacco model and understanding resources available to support a client at different stages.

The project also provides workshop sessions to community members. This involves a thorough explanation of the Yarning it Up – Don't Smoke it Up journey to quit tobacco model.

The workshops are culturally appropriate; education is presented as a story, which allows participants to lead the workshop.

Education workshops include:

- stages of change
- journey to quit model
- triggers and barriers
- referral process to Quitline
- types of supports available.

Source: Adapted from ACOSH (The Australian Council on Smoking and Health), 2018, <https://www.acosh.org/yarning-dont-smoke/>

Evaluate the capacity of the Yarning it Up – Don't Smoke it Up program to improve health outcomes for Aboriginal and Torres Strait Islander people.

Question 9 (6 marks)

Consider the following two sources relating to life expectancy.

Source 1

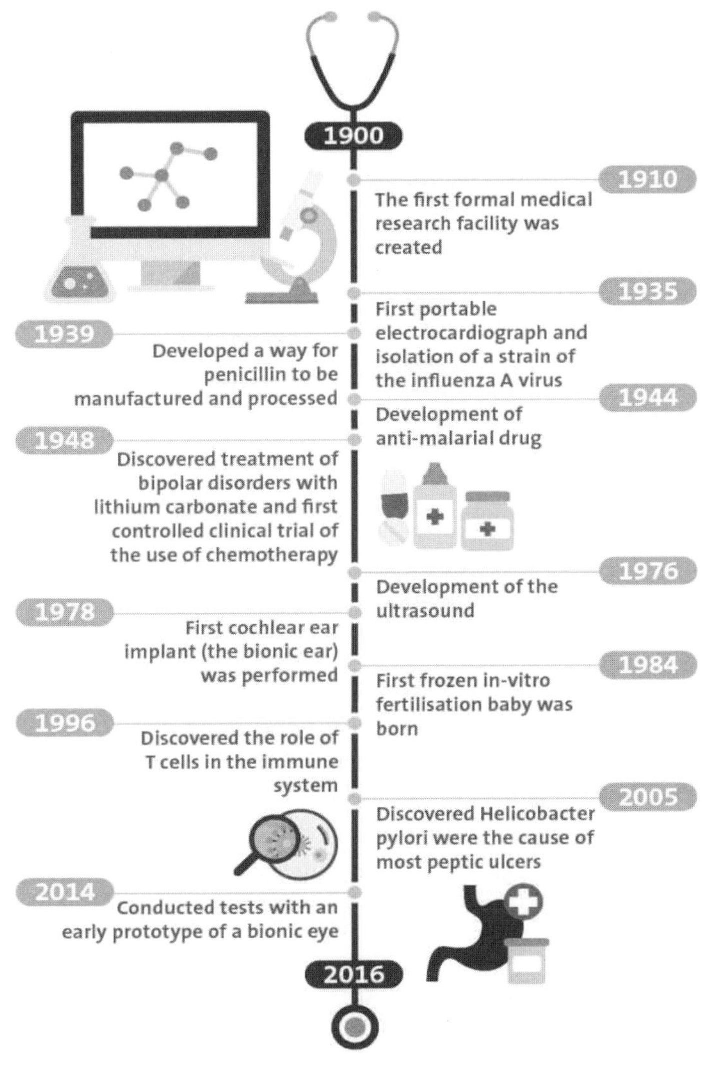

Source: 'The past, present and future of our health tech', Compare the Market, <https://www.comparethemarket.com.au/blog/health/past-present-future-health-tech/>, 13 March 2018

Source 2

The following data is from the Australian Bureau of Statistics.

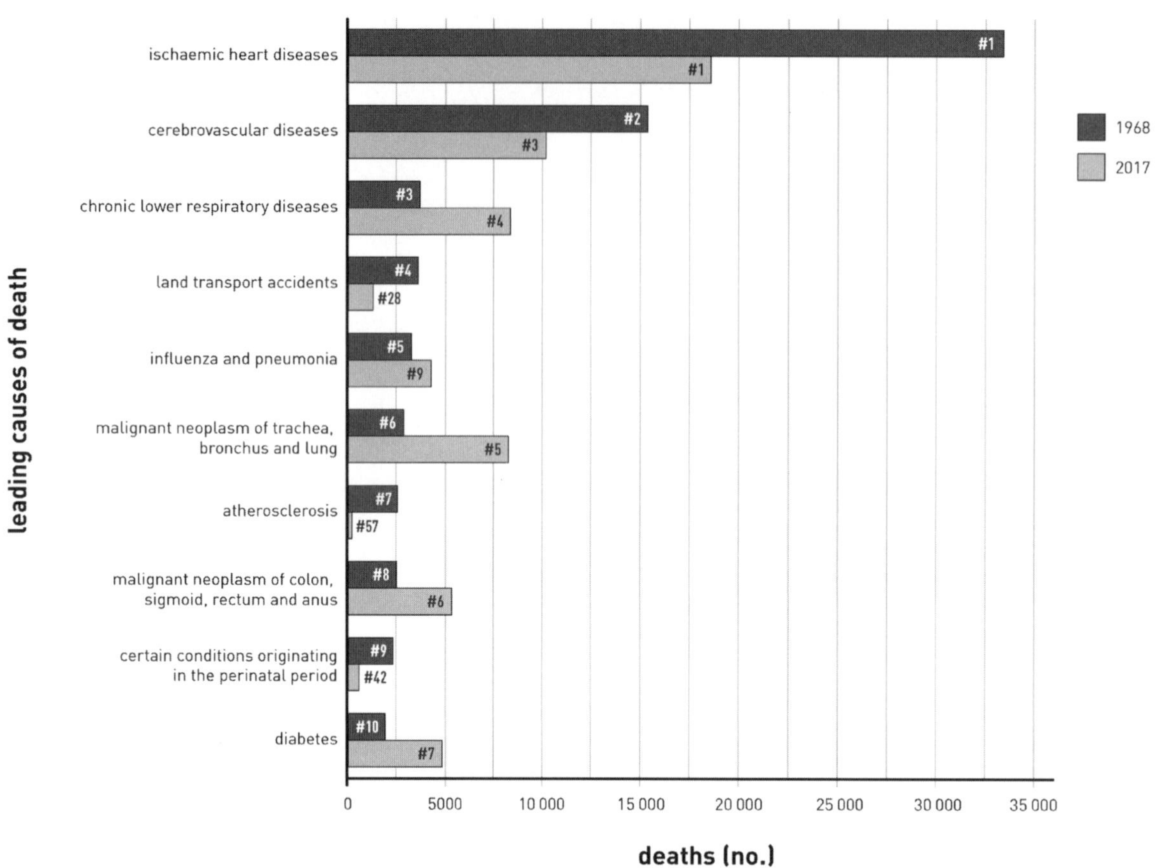

Source: Australian Bureau of Statistics (1968–2017), 'Changing Patterns of Mortality in Australia', <https://www.abs.gov.au/statistics/health/causes-death/changing-patterns-mortality-australia/latest-release>, accessed 24 July 2024; © Commonwealth of Australia, licensed under Creative Commons Attribution 4.0 International, <https://creativecommons.org/licenses/by/4.0/legalcode.en>

Using the information provided, analyse the extent to which 'old' public health, the biomedical model of health and the social model of health have helped to improve life expectancy in Australia between 1968 and 2017.

Question 10 (6 marks)

a. Explain the relationship between the Australian Dietary Guidelines and the Australian Guide to Healthy Eating. 2 marks

b. Discuss the role that either the Australian Dietary Guidelines or the Australian Guide to Healthy Eating could play in decreasing the impact of **one** dietary risk on Australia's health outcomes. 4 marks

Question 11 (4 marks)

Using **one** of the programs below, explain how the social model of health is improving the health status of Australians.

Smoking: Quit program	The Quit program has worked hard to phase out tobacco advertising on television and radio. It has also encouraged changes to laws regarding plain packaging and non-smoking areas, and has a Quitline that offers support and advice for those trying to give up smoking.
Skin cancer: SunSmart program	The SunSmart program encourages schools to have policies such as 'no hat, no play' and advocates for shade when planning outdoor spaces. SunSmart also has an app that informs people of the UV levels for the day and a catchy slogan, 'slip, slop, slap, seek and slide', which encourages people to slip on a shirt, slop on some sunscreen, slap on a hat, seek shade and slide on sunglasses.
Road safety: Driver Reviver program	The Driver Reviver program opens up to 220 Driver Reviver sites across Australia each holiday season. These are located along popular routes and offer places for drivers to stop and refresh, with free tea, coffee, snacks and toilet facilities. The Driver Reviver program involves volunteers from the State Emergency Service (SES), Country Fire Authority (CFA) and Lions Club. It also has tips online for driving safely.

Question 12 (10 marks)

The Australian Government allocates a significant amount of the yearly budget to healthcare, particularly towards Medicare and the Pharmaceutical Benefits Scheme (PBS). Summaries of Medicare and PBS statistics for the 2017–18 financial year are shown below.

Source 1

More GP attendances and more benefits paid

In 2017–18, patients accessed almost 155 million GP services, at a cost in Medicare benefits of $7.8 billion. This compares to 149 million services in 2016–17 at a cost of $7.5 billion in Medicare benefits. This is an increase of 4.9% in service volume and an increase in benefits of 5.5% compared with 2016–17.

More Medicare services overall

The volume of total Medicare services in 2017–18 was 414.3 million services, at a cost of $23.2 billion in Medicare benefits. This compares to 394.3 million services 2016–17, at a cost of $22.0 billion in Medicare benefits. This is an increase of 5.9% in service volume and an increase in benefits of 6.3% compared with 2016–17.

Source: © Commonwealth of Australia, <http://www.health.gov.au/internet/main/publishing.nsf/Content/Annual-Medicare-Statistics>

Source 2

Total Pharmaceutical Benefits Scheme (PBS) government expenditure (both Section 85 and Section 100) on an accrual accounting basis for the 2017–18 financial year was $11 690 million (excluding revenue), compared with $12 058 million for the previous year. This is a decrease of 3.0%.

Total 2017–18 PBS subsidised prescription volume increased by 0.8% to a total of 204.1 million, compared to 202.4 million for the 2016–17 financial year.

In 2017–18, PBS government expenditure (Section 85 and Section 100) was $11 602.9 million (excluding rebates), which is 88.9% of the total cost of PBS prescriptions. The remainder was patient contributions, which amounted to $1 455.5 million.

Source: Pharmaceutical Benefits Scheme (PBS), <http://www.pbs.gov.au/info/statistics/expenditure-prescriptions/expenditure-prescriptions-twelve-months-to-30-june-2018>, accessed 24 March 2019

a. Using the information above, explain how the PBS may promote health and wellbeing and improve Australia's health status. 6 marks

b. Private health insurance is another form of health cover in Australia.

Explain the difference between private health insurance and Medicare. In your response, consider sustainability and funding. 4 marks

Question 13 (3 marks)

Identify **one** Australian Dietary Guideline that has been developed to address high intake of fat, salt and sugar, and outline the contribution this guideline has on the health outcomes of Australians.

Question 14 (10 marks)

Consider the following three sources relating to obesity and the challenges in bringing about dietary change.

Source 1

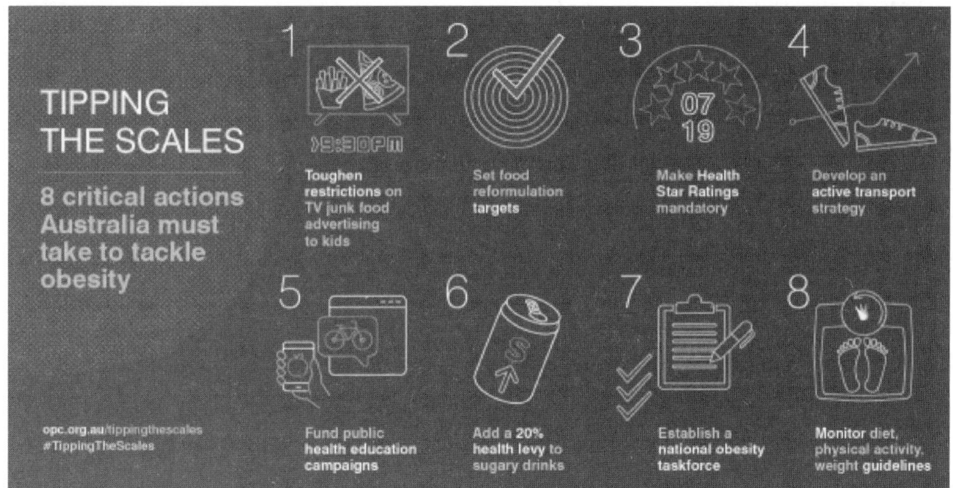

Source: Food for Health Alliance (previously Obesity Policy Coalition), 'Tipping the Scales', <https://www.foodforhealthalliance.org.au/what-we-do/national-international-strategies/tipping-the-scales.html>; reproduced with permission by Cancer Council Victoria

Source 2

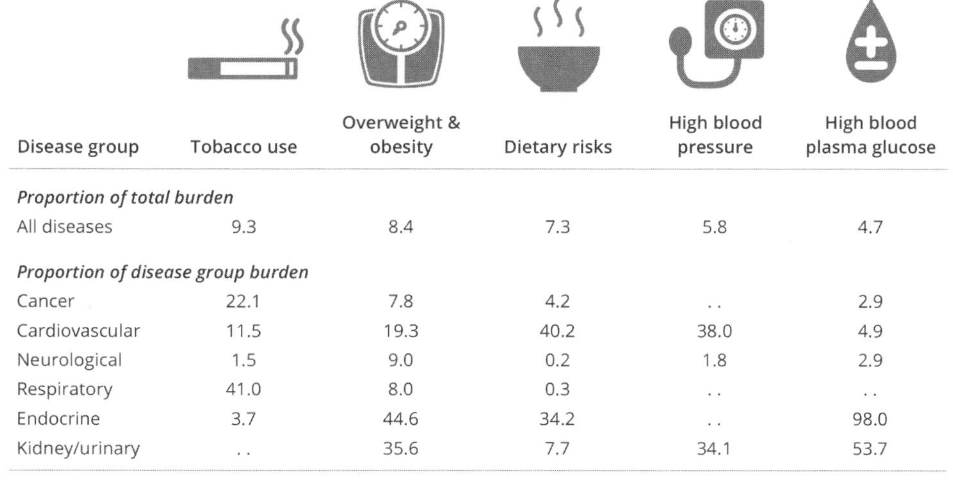

Table 1: Proportion (%) of total burden (DALY) attributable to the leading risk factors, for selected disease groups, 2015

Disease group	Tobacco use	Overweight & obesity	Dietary risks	High blood pressure	High blood plasma glucose
Proportion of total burden					
All diseases	9.3	8.4	7.3	5.8	4.7
Proportion of disease group burden					
Cancer	22.1	7.8	4.2	. .	2.9
Cardiovascular	11.5	19.3	40.2	38.0	4.9
Neurological	1.5	9.0	0.2	1.8	2.9
Respiratory	41.0	8.0	0.3	. .	. .
Endocrine	3.7	44.6	34.2	. .	98.0
Kidney/urinary	. .	35.6	7.7	34.1	53.7

Notes

1. Estimates for diet are based on an analysis of the joint effects of all dietary risk factors included in the study following methods used in recent global burden of disease studies.
2. Blank cells '. .' indicate that the risk factor has no associated diseases or injuries in the disease group.

Source: Australian Institute of Health and Welfare (AIHW), 'Australian Burden of Disease Study: Impact and Causes of Illness and Disease in Australia 2015 Summary Report', p. 10, <www.aihw.gov.au/getmedia/08eb5dd0-a7c0-429a-b35f-c8275e7a1dbf/aihw-bod-21.pdf.aspx?inline=true>; licensed under Creative Commons Attribution 3.0 Unported, <https://creativecommons.org/licenses/by/3.0/legalcode.en>

Source 3

Pick'n'Mix 1-6

For a healthy lunchbox pick & mix something from each food group 1 – 6!

The Department of Health Pick & Mix 1-6 poster provides a range of ideas and practical tips to inspire families to create healthy school lunchboxes.

Pick and mix one tasty option from each of the five core food groups to create a healthy lunchbox every day:

1. **Fruit** (e.g. fresh, frozen, pureed and canned in natural juice)
2. **Vegetables, legumes and beans**
3. **Milk, yoghurt, cheese and alternatives**
4. **Lean meats and poultry, fish, eggs, tofu, nuts and seeds, and legumes/beans**
5. **Grain** (cereal) foods
6. **Plain water**

Source: 'Healthy lunchboxes', <https://heas.health.vic.gov.au/resources/food-drink-ideas/healthy-lunchboxes/>. This resource was produced by the Healthy Eating Advisory Service, delivered by Nutrition Australia – Vic Division, with support from the Victorian Government. Copyright © State of Victoria.

Using the information provided and your understanding of healthy eating initiatives promoted in Australia, draw conclusions regarding Australians' ability to increase healthy eating. Consider the health status of Australians and the improvements that could be achieved.

Question 15 (6 marks)

Samoa, an island in the South Pacific, has had an outbreak of measles.

Explain how 'old' public health, the biomedical model of health and the social model of health could be used by Samoa to manage the spread of the measles disease.

Question 16 (14 marks)

Below is a section of an article that appeared on the BreastScreen Victoria website in 2019.

The Aboriginal Breast Screening Shawl Trial

Aboriginal women have reported a lack of cultural awareness among health professionals, fear, shame and logistical barriers as negative impacts of screening. To address these barriers, in 2018, we developed the Aboriginal Breast Screening Shawl Trial. The Victorian Aboriginal Community Controlled Health Organisation (VACCHO) and the Victorian Aboriginal Health Service (VAHS) led this project and ensured that Aboriginal Community Control was central at every stage.

The shawls were made for Aboriginal women in the trial to wear during their breast screen. They are a culturally safe alternative to being naked from the waist up or asking for a standard screening gown. The shawls aim to improve Aboriginal women's experience with breast screening. Other objectives were to support Aboriginal women to screen together as a group and to increase the cultural competence of BreastScreen Victoria staff.

The original shawl used in the trial featured detailed artwork by respected Wiradjuri and Yorta Yorta artist Lynnette Briggs. She was inspired by the many stories of women and their personal journeys they shared in yarning circles.

This week, the Aboriginal Breast Screening Shawl Trial won a 2019 VicHealth Award in the category of Improving Health Equity. Congratulations and thank you to everyone who worked on this fantastic project: Annie Cooper, Monique Warrillow, Mel Davis, and Lisa Joyce. And to our partners: VACCHO, VAHS, Department of Health and Human Services, Deakin University, Cancer Council Victoria, St Vincent's Hospital BreastScreen clinic, Western Health and Women's Health West.

The shawls go on the road with the mobile screening service

The success of the trial led us to roll it out across Victoria. In October and November, our mobile screening service visited seven Aboriginal Community Controlled Organisations (ACCOs). Women who screened received a shawl.

The project has been an enormous success. One hundred and sixty Aboriginal women screened, a significant achievement for an under-screened group. 82% of the women who screened were new to breast screening or had lapsed. That is, they had screened before but had not returned within the recommended two-year period. The experience was overwhelmingly positive, with 82% of women agreeing that the shawl made them feel culturally safe. 95% of women agreed that they felt more comfortable screening because the mobile screening service was located at their local Aboriginal health service.

Source: Adapted from BreastScreen Victoria, 'Improving Screening for Aboriginal Women', 4 December 2019, <www.breastscreen.org.au/news/improving-screening-for-aboriginal-women/>; reproduced with permission from BreastScreen Victoria

a. Define 'social justice'. 2 marks

b. Describe how the Aboriginal Breast Screening Shawl Trial promotes social justice. 2 marks

c. Explain two ways the social model of health is reflected in the breast screening initiative to promote health and wellbeing. 4 marks

1.

2.

d. Evaluate the effectiveness of the Aboriginal Breast Screening Shawl Trial in improving health and wellbeing for Aboriginal people. 6 marks

Question 17 (6 marks)

a. Describe Medicare. 2 marks

b. Explain how Medicare and the National Disability Insurance Scheme (NDIS) promote health and wellbeing in Australia by providing access. 4 marks

Unit 4 | Area of Study 1 Global health and human development

Question 1 (5 marks)

Consider the following graphs.

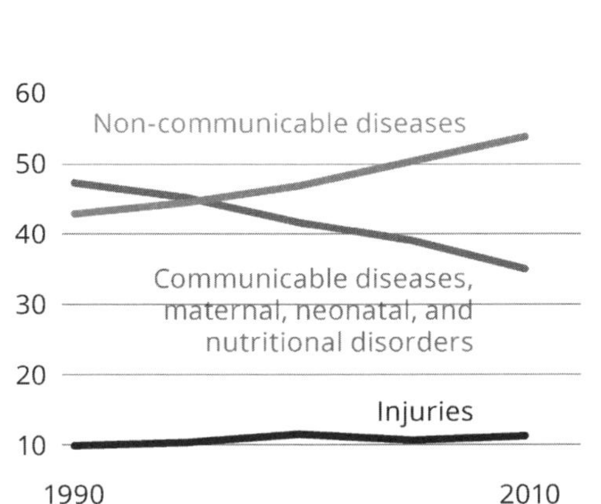

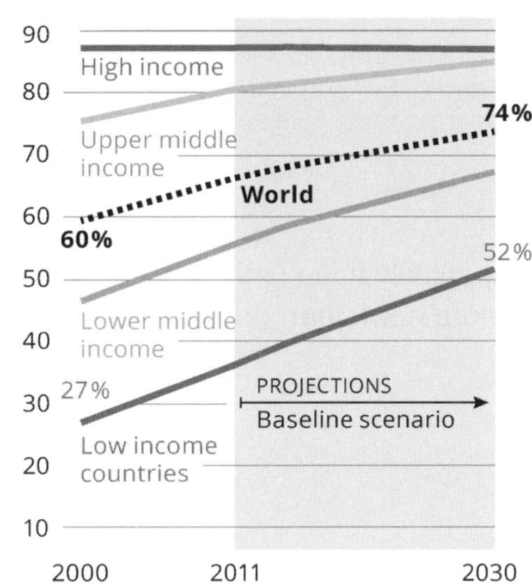

Source: European Environment Agency, 'The shift in global disease burden, and share of non-communicable diseases by world regions', <https://www.eea.europa.eu/data-and-maps/figures/the-shift-in-global-disease>, updated 23 February 2017

a. Outline **one** trend evident in either of the graphs above. 1 mark

b. Based on the data, outline one similarity and one difference in the health status in low-, lower middle- and upper middle-income countries. 2 marks

Similarity

Difference

c. Explain **one** factor that could contribute to the trend identified in **part a.** 2 marks

Question 2 (6 marks)

'While digital technology initially had significant benefits for global health and wellbeing, ultimately it will cause more harm than good.'

Evaluate this statement.

Question 3 (6 marks)

The table below shows the level of human development and the Human Development Index (HDI) of several countries.

Country	Level of human development	Human Development Index
Australia	very high	0.938
China	high	0.758
India	medium	0.647
Papua New Guinea	low	0.543

Data: United Nations Development Programme, International Human Development Indicators, http://hdr.undp.org/en/countries. Disclaimer: this data set has since been updated, and this does not reflect current information.

Using your understanding of the concept of human development and the data above, evaluate the use of the Human Development Index in measuring and comparing countries.

Question 4 (5 marks)

a. Identify **two** characteristics of a low-income country. 2 marks

b. Explain how **one** of the characteristics outlined in **part a.** would affect a country's burden of disease. 3 marks

Question 5 (4 marks)

Australia has a very low prevalence of human immunodeficiency virus (HIV) compared to many middle- and low-income countries.

Explain **two** factors that could account for this difference.

Question 6 (8 marks)

Consider the following three sources relating to the effect of processed foods on health.

Source 1

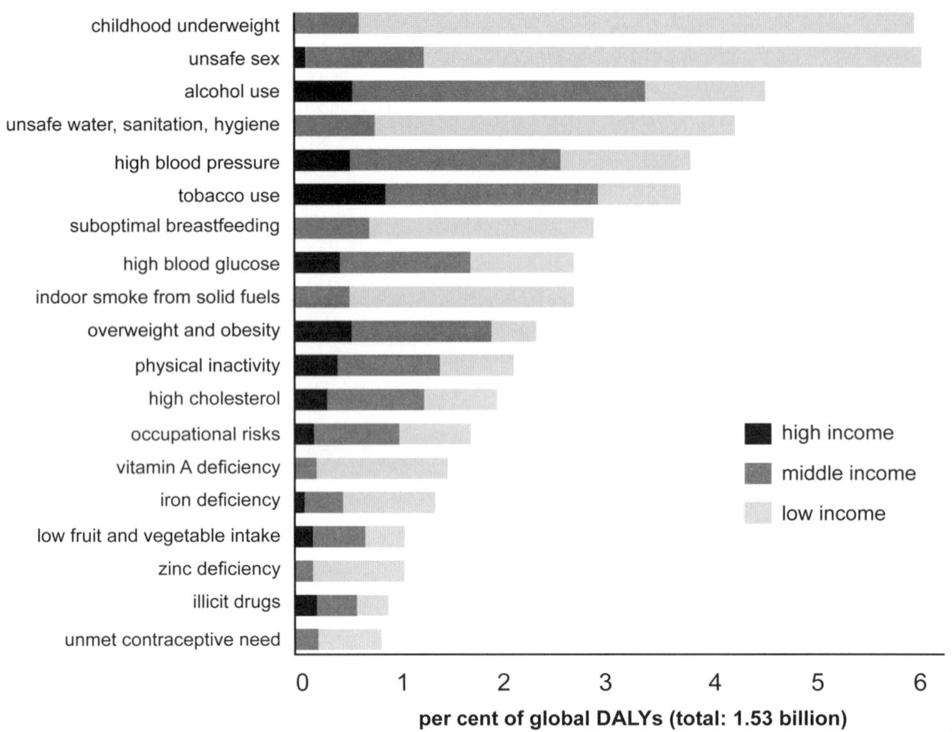

Source: Sanjay Basu, 'Alcohol use around the globe: new data trends', EpiAnalysis, <https://epianalysis.wordpress.com/2012/02/28/alcohol/>, 28 February 2012, posted under a Creative Commons Attribution-Share Alike 3.0 license. Full terms at <https://creativecommons.org/licenses/by-sa/3.0/deed.en>

Source 2

FIG. 3. PERCENTAGE OF POPULATION WITH BEST-PRACTICE POLICIES IN EFFECT OR PASSED, BY COUNTRY INCOME LEVEL

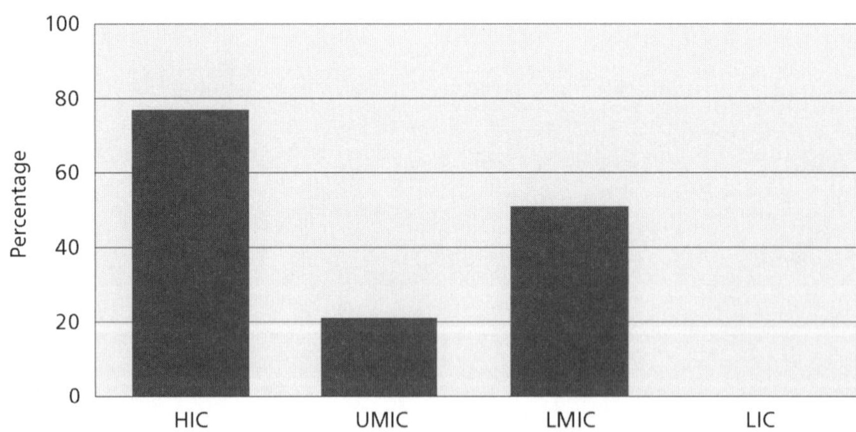

HIC: high-income countries; LIC: low-income countries; LMIC: lower-middle-income countries; UMIC: upper- middle-income countries (using World Bank country classifications by income level, 2022–2023; https://datahelpdesk.worldbank.org/knowledgebase/articles/906519-world-bank-country-and-lending-groups).

Source: 'Countdown to 2023: WHO report on global trans-fat elimination 2022', Geneva: World Health Organization, <https://iris.who.int/bitstream/handle/10665/365617/9789240067233-eng.pdf>, 2023; licensed under CC BY-NC-SA 3.0 IGO, <https://creativecommons.org/licenses/by-nc-sa/3.0/igo/legalcode.en>

Source 3

The following article was published on *The Conversation* in 2021.

How big companies are targeting middle income countries to boost ultra processed food sales

Ultra-processed foods might not be a familiar term to many people. But it is an emerging, and increasingly dominant type of food in the world. They are foods typically created through a 'series of industrial techniques and processes'.

They are designed to be potentially more addictive. They are also hyper-palatable, meaning that they can create a 'highly rewarding eating experience that may facilitate overconsumption'. And they are heavily marketed products, such as soft drinks, instant noodles and baby formula.

Ultra-processed foods are often high in calories, added sugars, trans-fats, and sodium. They also undergo extensive industrial processing and often contain many artificial additives. This makes them harmful to health. Their consumption is associated with higher risks of obesity, cardiovascular disease, type 2 diabetes, certain cancers, and other noncommunicable diseases (NCDs).

Ultra-processed foods consumption is already high. But it is unlikely to increase further in high-income countries like Australia and the US where sales have peaked. This means that corporations producing these products are rapidly expanding their operations in industrialising countries. Examples include South Africa, Indonesia, China and Brazil. This raises major concerns for global public health, given that these countries represent the bulk of the world's population.

In our recently published study, we find that total sales of ultra-processed foods in these industrialising countries will be equivalent to those in rich countries by 2024. These projected expansions of Big Food and ultra-processed food markets in middle income countries raises major concerns about the global capacity to prevent and treat NCDs.

Source: Adapted from Edwin Kwong (University of Melbourne), Joanna Williams (Swinburne University of Technology), Phillip Baker (Deakin University), Rob Moodie (University of Melbourne), Thiago M Santos (Federal University of Pelotas), 'How big companies are targeting middle income countries to boost ultra-processed food sales', *The Conversation*, https://theconversation.com/how-big-companies-are-targeting-middle-income-countries-to-boost-ultra-processed-food-sales-166927; licensed under Creative Commons Attribution/No Derivatives 4.0 International, <https://creativecommons.org/licenses/by-nd/4.0/legalcode.en>

Using the information provided, analyse the impact of the global marketing of processed foods on health and wellbeing in high-income, middle-income and low-income countries.

Question 7 (9 marks)

Human Development Index 2016 – Highest rankings

HDI ranking	Country	Human Development Index (HDI)	Life expectancy at birth	Expected years of schooling	Mean years of schooling	Gross national income (GNI) per capita
1	Norway	0.949	81.7	17.7	12.7	67,614
2	Australia	0.939	82.5	20.4	13.2	42,822
2	Switzerland	0.939	83.1	16.0	13.4	56,364
4	Germany	0.926	81.1	17.1	13.2	45,000
5	Singapore	0.925	83.2	15.4	11.6	78,162
5	Denmark	0.925	80.4	19.2	12.7	44,519
7	Netherlands	0.924	81.7	18.1	11.9	46,326
8	Ireland	0.923	81.1	18.6	12.3	43,798
9	Iceland	0.921	82.7	19.0	12.2	37,065
10	Canada	0.920	82.2	16.3	13.1	42,582
10	United States	0.920	79.2	16.5	13.2	53,245
12	Hong Kong, China (SAR)	0.917	84.2	15.7	11.6	54,265
13	New Zealand	0.915	82.0	19.2	12.5	32,870
14	Sweden	0.913	82.3	16.1	12.3	46,251
15	Liechtenstein	0.912	80.2	14.6	12.4	75,065
16	United Kingdom	0.909	80.8	16.3	13.3	37,931

Source: UNDP (United Nations Development Programme), 'Human Development Report 2016: Human Development for Everyone', 2016, <https://hdr.undp.org/content/human-development-report-2016>, p.198; licensed under Creative Commons Attribution 3.0, <https://creativecommons.org/licenses/by/3.0/igo/legalcode>

The table above depicts the four indicators used to measure a country's Human Development Index (HDI).

a. What are the dimensions of the HDI? 3 marks

b. Which organisation is responsible for producing the HDI? 1 mark

c. 'Norway clearly has the highest level of human development in the world because it is ranked number one on the HDI.'

To what extent do you agree with this statement? 5 marks

Question 8 (3 marks)

Explain how environmental sustainability promotes physical health and wellbeing in a global context.

Question 9 (2 marks)

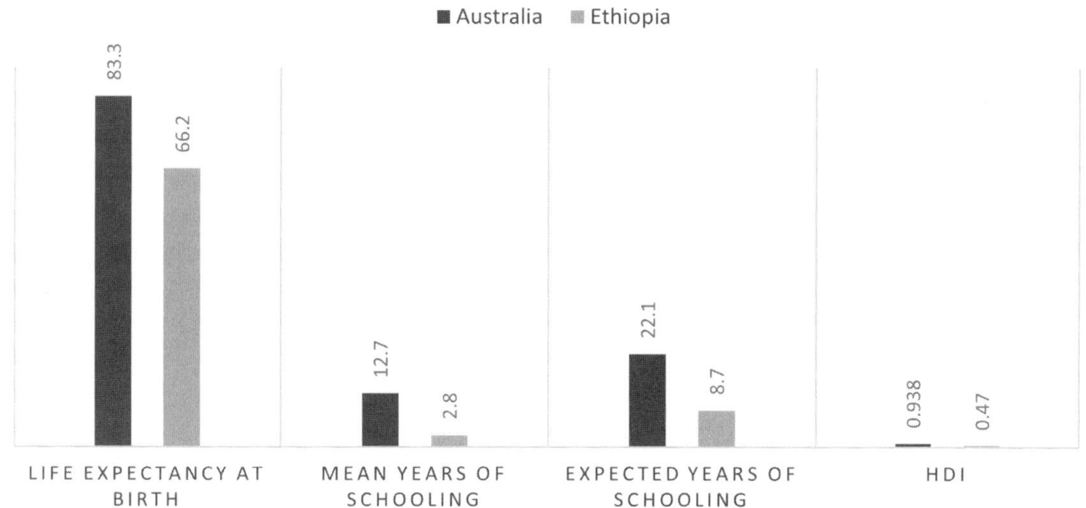

Source: Adapted from United Nations Development Programme, 'UN Human Development Report 2019, Beyond income, beyond averages, beyond today: Inequalities in human development in the 21st century', 2019, pp. 300 and 302, <https://hdr.undp.org/content/human-development-report-2019>; licensed under Creative Commons Attribution 3.0 Intergovernmental Organisation, <https://creativecommons.org/licenses/by/3.0/igo/legalcode>

Use the information in the graph to explain the differences in the HDI between Australia and Ethiopia.

Question 10 (3 marks)

Outline a characteristic that is common for high-, middle- and low-income countries.

High-income country

Middle-income country

Low-income country

Question 11 (4 marks)

An article was published on 6 December 2019 by the World Economic Forum with the title 'The Cost of the Climate Crisis? 20 Million Homeless Every Year.'

Describe the implications of climate change and mass migration on health and wellbeing.

Question 12 (5 marks)

Consider the following data.

Country	Human Rights Index
Australia	0.93
South Sudan	0.17
India	0.57

Source: Our World in Data, 'Human Rights Index, 2023' (data adapted from V-Dem), <https://ourworldindata.org/grapher/human-rights-index-vdem>

a. Describe social sustainability. 2 marks

b. Use the data in the table above to explain how social sustainability can impact on human development. 3 marks

Unit 4 | Area of Study 2 Health and the Sustainable Development Goals

Question 1 (10 marks)

Source: From 'SDG 3: Good Health And Well-Being', by United Nations in India, © 2017 United Nations. <http://in.one.un.org/page/sustainable-development-goals/sdg-3-2/>, accessed 2018. Reprinted with the permission of the United Nations

a. Who is responsible for the Sustainable Development Goals (SDGs)? 1 mark

b. Describe the importance of the SDGs for human development. 3 marks

c. Explain the relationship between the following SDGs in improving health and human development globally. 6 marks

SDGs 3 and 12

SDGs 3 and 4

Question 2 (3 marks)

Describe an effective non-government aid program aimed at increasing health and human development. In your description include the:

- SDG addressed
- purpose of the program
- partnerships involved in the program.

Question 3 (8 marks)

a. Identify **two** key features of SDG 3, Ensure healthy lives and promote wellbeing for all at all ages. 2 marks

b. Explain how actions taken to achieve SDG 1, End poverty in all its forms everywhere, could assist in achieving SDG 3. 3 marks

c. Explain how achieving SDG 3 promotes sustainability. 3 marks

Question 4 (5 marks)

Papua New Guinea (PNG) and Australia: a broad and enduring partnership

- 560 Australia Award Scholarships 2018, 60% of which were awarded to women
- 3000 legal and support officers trained
- $6 billion worth of two-way trade in 2017
- Around 5000 Australian businesses operate in PNG investing over $16 billion into PNG economy

Source: Adapted from: Australian Government Department of Foreign Affairs and Trade, 'Papua New Guinea and Australia: A Broad and Enduring Partnership', <https://dfat.gov.au/geo/papua-new-guinea/development-assistance/Documents/papua-new-guinea-and-australia-a-broad-and-enduring-partnership-infographic.pdf>

a. Identify and describe the type of aid evident in the assistance programs above. 2 marks

b. Identify **two** reasons why Australia would provide significant aid to Papua New Guinea. 2 marks

Question 5 (9 marks)

afao AUSTRALIAN FEDERATION OF AIDS ORGANISATIONS

HIV in Australia: 2017

Key statistics

1,065 (2012) 1,030 (2013) 1,082 (2014) 1,025 (2015)

Following a rise in HIV in 2012, **new HIV diagnoses have stabilised** over the years 2012–2015.

Of the estimated **25,313 HIV-positive people** in Australia at the end of 2015, around **2,619 (10%)** were unaware of their status.

The stabilisation of new diagnoses since 2012 comes after years of increased HIV testing alongside efforts to encourage **earlier access to HIV treatments**.

In 2015, 29% of new HIV diagnoses were **diagnosed late**, emphasising the ongoing importance of **regular HIV testing**.

Highly effective HIV treatment means that **AIDS death and illnesses are now rare**.

Source: Australian Federation of AIDS Organisations (AFAO), 'HIV in Australia: 2017', 2017, <https://www.afao.org.au/wp-content/uploads/2017/04/HIV-in-Australia-2017.pdf>

Australia has a very low prevalence of HIV compared to many middle- and low-income countries.

The Global Fund to Fight AIDS, Tuberculosis and Malaria is a program that aims to reduce the incidence of HIV worldwide. The program aims to set up and work with local health clinics and health services. The Global Fund works in conjunction with UNAIDS, World Vision and other non-government organisations. They provide AIDS and safe-sex education programs to schools and communities. Condom use is encouraged, and condoms are distributed for free. The program offers free STI and HIV/AIDS testing and treatment, as well as counselling sessions for those diagnosed.

a. What type of aid is evident in the Global Fund program? 1 mark

b. Evaluate the effectiveness of the Global Fund program. 4 marks

c. Explain how the priority of the World Health Organization (WHO) 'Power health' could be used to address the spread of HIV. 2 marks

d. Outline **two** examples of social action that could be applied to address the spread of HIV. 2 marks

Question 6 (6 marks)

In an historic announcement on World Polio Day, an independent commission of experts concluded that wild poliovirus type 3 (WPV3) has been eradicated worldwide. Following the eradication of smallpox and wild poliovirus type 2, this news represents a historic achievement for humanity.

Source: World Health Organization, 'Two Out of Three Wild Poliovirus Strains Eradicated' <www.who.int/news-room/feature-stories/detail/two-out-of-three-wild-poliovirus-strains-eradicated>; viewed 16 January 2020

a. List three of the main components of the goal of the World Health Organization (WHO). 3 marks

1.

2.

3.

b. Identify **one** of the WHO priorities given in **part a.** and explain how it makes the announcement on World Polio Day possible. 3 marks

Question 7 (9 marks)

> Elisa and fellow midwives from Melbourne raised funds to travel to Ethiopia and volunteer as midwives at the local hospital. They sought donations by setting up a fundraising webpage and informing people on social media about their opportunity to volunteer. In Ethiopia, they volunteered with a local hospital to assist in the delivery of babies. While there, they provided education to the midwives on procedures to support women during the birth process. They used the money to purchase much-needed equipment to support the midwives and doctors in the Ethiopian hospital to support a successful delivery.

a. Outline **two** key features of Sustainable Development Goal (SDG) 3, Ensure healthy lives and promote wellbeing for all at all ages, that are evident in the work of Elisa and the midwives from Melbourne. 2 marks

b. **i.** Identify an SDG other than SDG 3 that is reflected in the information above. 1 mark

ii. Explain how work completed for the SDG identified in **part b.i.** relates to SDG 3 and can assist in improving health and wellbeing and human development globally. Use examples from the case study to support your answer. 6 marks

Question 8 (4 marks)

Volunteering is a type of social action.

Describe **two** other types of social action that a person may take to address SDG 3.

Question 9 (4 marks)

An article was published on 6 December 2019 by the World Economic Forum with the title 'The Cost of the Climate Crisis? 20 Million Homeless Every Year.'

Using an example, explain how a non-government organisation operating in Australia could promote health and wellbeing and human development globally for the people displaced by climate change.

Question 10 (3 marks)

Identify and describe **one** type of aid that the Australian Government could provide to populations impacted by conflict.

SAMPLE RESPONSES

Question 1a.

Sample response

Spiritual health and wellbeing is not material in nature, but relates to ideas, beliefs, values and ethics that arise in the minds and consciences of human beings. It includes the concepts of hope, peace, a guiding sense of meaning or value, and reflecting on one's place in the world. Spiritual health and wellbeing can be highly individualised; for example, in some spiritual traditions health may relate to organised religion, a higher power and prayer. In other practices it can relate to morals, values, a sense of purpose in life, connection or belonging.

Mark allocation: 2 marks

- 1 mark for each of the following: ideas or beliefs; values or ethics; sense of purpose in life; connection or belonging (up to 2 marks)

TIP

» **You will not be asked to define the dimensions of health and wellbeing but you must be able to describe them using key words.**

Question 1b.

Sample response

When a young person plays sport, they are more likely to be able to maintain a healthy body weight and participate regularly in physical activity (physical health and wellbeing); this allows the young person to complete daily tasks including attending school. When a young person attends school, they can learn new knowledge (mental health and wellbeing) and be able to use logic to make good decisions affecting their life; these can be used in their sports but also in their broader life experiences, leading to a young person feeling content and happy with their life (emotional health and wellbeing). When a young person is content and can positively express their emotions, people will be open to forming meaningful relationships with them (social health and wellbeing) and appreciate the effective communication of emotions. When young people have meaningful connections in their life through playing sport and attending school, they feel a connection and sense of belonging in their life, promoting spiritual health and wellbeing.

Mark allocation: 5 marks

- 1 mark for an appropriate example used to explain the links that exist between dimensions
- 1 mark per relationship explained between two dimensions of health and wellbeing (up to 4 marks)

Note: 'Health and wellbeing' is a positive concept so students will not gain full marks if they refer to negative health and wellbeing outcomes in their response.

Question 1c.

Sample response

Possible responses are outlined in the table below.

Individual	National	Global
• work productively • gain an education • earn an income • regularly exercise • effectively run a household (e.g. shopping, cleaning, caring for children) • spend time with friends • work towards a purpose in life • increase leisure time • live independently • sleep well • maintain positive thought patterns	• economic benefits • increased productivity, less absenteeism from work • higher average incomes • fewer people relying on social security • health system savings, more money spent on education • social benefits • increased social participation • reduced stress and anxiety in the community • longer, healthier lives and increased life expectancy	• promotes social development • promotes economic development • assists in promoting peace and stability • promotes sustainability • reduces risk of disease transmission between countries

Mark allocation: 3 marks

- 1 mark for outlining one way optimal health and wellbeing can act as a resource at an individual level
- 1 mark for outlining one way optimal health and wellbeing can act as a resource at a national level
- 1 mark for outlining one way optimal health and wellbeing can act as a resource at a global level

Question 2

Sample response

> The Quit program decreasing the number of people smoking may lead to a lower incidence of lung cancer and respiratory diseases, improving the functioning of an individual's body and its systems. This means that, at the individual level, there is an increase in a person's ability to work and earn an income because they are not sick from smoking-related conditions.
>
> Smoking can compromise an individual's immune system, and the Quit program encourages people to quit smoking using the Quitline. This leads to having fewer smokers in the country, leading to increased productivity due to people not needing to take as much time off work, and increased economic benefits to the nation as less money is spent on paying for sick days.

Mark allocation: 4 marks

- 2 marks for linking a program to health and wellbeing as an individual resource (examples include working productively, gaining an education, earning an income, exercising, effectively running a household, spending time with friends, working towards their purpose in life, increasing leisure time, living independently, sleeping well and maintaining positive thought patterns)
- 2 marks for linking a program to health and wellbeing as a national resource (examples include economic benefits, increased productivity, less absenteeism from work, higher average incomes, fewer people relying on social security, health system savings, more money being spent on education, social benefits, increased social participation, reduced stress and anxiety in the community, longer and healthier lives, and increased life expectancy)

Question 3a.

Sample response

Life expectancy is an indication of how long a person can expect to live if death rates do not change.

Mark allocation: 1 mark

- 1 mark for accurately outlining what is meant by life expectancy

TIP

» **You need to be able to outline or explain health status indicators, using key words from their definitions.**

Question 3b.

Sample response

Environmental factor: Men are more likely to work in dangerous work environments (e.g. with machinery) compared to women. This can increase their risk of having accidents at work, which may lead to premature death and a decreased life expectancy.

Biological factor: Women are more likely to have higher levels of oestrogen compared to men, which can be protective against cardiovascular disease (CVD). Therefore, women are less likely to develop or die prematurely from CVD, which increases their life expectancy compared to men.

Mark allocation: 4 marks

- 1 mark for outlining an environmental factor
- 1 mark for outlining a biological factor
- 1 mark for providing a link between the environmental factor and differences in life expectancy between men and women
- 1 mark for providing a link between the biological factor and differences in life expectancy between men and women

Note: When an exam question specifically says 'the difference between men and women', the response would need to include both men and women in order to get full marks.

TIP

» **You should know at least three examples of each type of factor. This ensures that you can pick the best example for the question.**

Question 3c.

Sample response

Access to health information: As the access to information increases and there is a greater focus on men accessing health information, more men may use preventative measures and seek help earlier. This could result in fewer men dying prematurely, thereby increasing their life expectancy and moving it closer to that of women.

Mark allocation: 2 marks

- 1 mark for outlining a sociocultural factor
- 1 mark for showing a link between the factor and the decreasing gap between male and female life expectancies

Question 4a.

Sample response

> Emotional health is the degree to which you feel emotionally secure and relaxed in everyday life, as well as the ability to positively express feelings. This involves the positive management and expression of emotional actions and reactions as well as the ability to display resilience.

Mark allocation: 2 marks

- 1 mark for showing that emotional health and wellbeing relates to being able to express feelings in a positive way
- 1 mark for showing that emotional health and wellbeing relates to being able to display resilience

TIP

» **You should be able to describe all the dimensions of health and wellbeing.**

Question 4b.

Sample response

> While a person may have poor emotional health and wellbeing (e.g. low levels of resilience), they may still experience a high level of wellbeing, resulting in good overall health and wellbeing.
>
> For example, a person may have efficient functioning of the body (positive physical health and wellbeing), which could lead to an overall sense of good health and wellbeing.

Note: Other examples include having high self-esteem (positive mental health and wellbeing), having a sense of purpose (positive spiritual health and wellbeing) or having positive relationships (positive social health and wellbeing) despite having poor emotional health and wellbeing.

Mark allocation: 2 marks

- 1 mark for providing an example that shows what poor emotional health and wellbeing may look like
- 1 mark for explaining how good overall health and wellbeing can still occur regardless of poor emotional health and wellbeing

Question 5

Sample response

> Because a majority (97%) of Aboriginal and Torres Strait Islander peoples have an inadequate intake of fruit and vegetables, it is likely that they are lacking the nutrient fibre. A lack of fibre in your diet can lead to an increased risk of obesity, as fibre provides a feeling of satiety. Without this, one may choose to snack on energy-dense foods, which can increase the risk of obesity. Increased rates of obesity can lead to increased rates of morbidity and mortality from obesity-related conditions (e.g. cardiovascular disease), negatively impacting the health status of Aboriginal and Torres Strait Islander peoples.

Mark allocation: 3 marks

- 1 mark for linking a lack of fruit and vegetables to a nutrient
- 1 mark for an explanation of the nutrient's function
- 1 mark for providing a link back to Aboriginal and Torres Strait Islander peoples' health status

TIP

» **Make sure you link your answer back to the question being asked. In this instance you need to link back to the impact on health status of Aboriginal and Torres Strait Islander peoples.**

Question 6a.

Sample response

> 'Burden of disease' is a measure of the impact of diseases and injuries. It measures the gap between current health status and an ideal situation where everyone lives to old age free of disease and disability.

Mark allocation: 2 marks

- 1 mark for stating that burden of disease refers to the impact of disease and injury
- 1 mark for stating that burden of disease measures the gap between current health status and an ideal situation

Note: No mark is awarded for stating that burden of disease is measured in a unit called disability-adjusted life year (DALY).

TIP

» **You should know the exact wording of the key health status indicators as outlined in the Study Design.**

Question 6b.

Sample response

Years lived with disability (YLD) is the number of years of life lost due to disability (non-fatal), whereas years of life lost (YLL) is the number of years of life lost due to premature death (fatal).

Mark allocation: 2 marks

- 2 marks for outlining a difference between YLD (disability, non-fatal, morbidity) and YLL (premature death, fatal, mortality)

TIP

» **When asked for a difference between two concepts, you should include comparing words in your answer, such as 'whereas' or 'compared with'.**

Question 6c.

Sample response

One disease that may result in higher YLD than YLL is anxiety because it causes a sufferer to experience many days or years of ill health but does not usually cause death.

Mark allocation: 2 marks

- 1 mark for identifying a disease that causes significant morbidity compared with mortality
- 1 mark for explaining that the disease causes more years of life lost due to morbidity and ill health than years of life lost due to premature death

Note: Answers may include but are not limited to mental health disorders (e.g. depression, anxiety and anorexia) or Alzheimer's disease.

Question 7a.

Sample response

> People who live further from major cities experience a greater number of deaths per 100 000 people.

Mark allocation: 1 mark

- 1 mark for stating that the death rate increases the further one lives from a major city or that the death rate decreases the closer one lives to a major city

Question 7b.

Sample response

> Sociocultural factor: Unemployment. People who live further from major cities are more likely to be unemployed. This may result in having insufficient income to purchase nutritious food. Malnutrition can lead to an intake of energy-dense foods and therefore an increased risk of cardiovascular disease (CVD). Increased risk of CVD, especially for people who cannot afford preventive healthcare, can lead to premature death; overall, there will be more deaths per 100 000 people among those living in remote and very remote areas than among those living in major cities.
>
> Environmental factor: Working conditions. People living in remote and very remote areas are more likely to have jobs requiring manual labour (e.g. farming) than people living in major cities. This can lead to increased exposure to occupational risks (e.g. machinery accidents) that can result in premature deaths, increasing the deaths per 100 000 people for those living in remote or very remote areas.

Mark allocation: 4 marks

- 1 mark for identifying each factor (up to 2 marks)
- 1 mark for explaining how each factor is associated with remote living and a greater number of deaths (up to 2 marks)

TIPS

» **When asked to explain a factor, take a moment to consider as many factors as possible, then choose one to write about that you can explain in the most detail. This will give you the best opportunity to achieve full marks.**

» **The easiest factors to link to health differences between geographical areas are biological (low birth weight and body weight), sociocultural (unemployment and cultural influences) and environmental (urban design and infrastructure, and working conditions).**

Question 8

Sample response

Social health and wellbeing: Social health and wellbeing involves the use of communication skills to effectively communicate in different social settings. Individuals are able to form meaningful and long-lasting relationships that satisfy the needs of those involved in the relationship.

Physical health and wellbeing: Physical health and wellbeing relates to the functioning of the body and its systems; it includes the ability of an individual to perform daily tasks.

Mark allocation: 4 marks

- 2 marks per correct response for each dimension of health and wellbeing (up to 4 marks)

Question 9

Sample response

Mental health and wellbeing allows for individuals and communities to develop ideas and solve problems to issues that affect all of us. A person with optimal mental health and wellbeing can attend school or productively contribute to the workforce of a country. Countries where people experience low levels of stress and positive self-esteem are likely to have a strong workforce. This is a global resource as it leads to opportunities for trade between countries, improving the economic stability of a country, which leads to a reduction in poverty and rates of mortality and morbidity.

Mark allocation: 2 marks

- 1 mark for knowledge about mental health and wellbeing
- 1 mark for explaining this dimension of health and wellbeing as a resource globally

TIP

» **When answering 'global resource' questions, it can usually help to link to an individual resource first and then use that to link to a resource globally.**

Question 10a.

Sample response

Health-adjusted life expectancy (HALE) is the number of years in full health that a person can expect to live without reduced functioning; it considers the quality of life not just the quantity, unlike life expectancy.

Mark allocation: 2 marks

- 2 marks for two clear statements that it is more than a total life expectancy measure; it considers the quality of life, as it measures the amount of time expected to be in full health and takes into consideration the impact of ill health

Question 10b.

Sample response

Men and women living in remote areas have a lower life expectancy than men and women living in major cities. For example, men in remote and very remote regions will have a life expectancy of approximately 13 years in full health from 65 years of age and a further 5 years in ill health, whereas men living in major cities will live approximately 15 years in full health from 65 years of age and 5 years in ill health.

Mark allocation: 2 marks

- 1 mark for a correct response that considers the changes in statistics according to remoteness; must include reference to both men and women
- 1 mark for addressing the life expectancy experienced by the populations, including correctly understanding that ill health and full health of HALE are addressed within the life expectancy measure

TIP

» **This question has asked for data; therefore, you must use some figures from the graph in your answer to gain full marks. Also, use the title of the graph and the measures of the axes to ensure you are using the data correctly in your answer.**

Question 11a.

Sample response

Between 2010 and 2019 all areas have seen a decrease in daily smoking.

Remote and very remote areas have consistently had the highest daily smoking percentages compared to other areas between 2010 and 2019.

Mark allocation: 2 marks

- 1 mark per correct trend (up to 2 marks)

Note: A trend is a pattern occurring over a period of time; students cannot use one moment in time and pick a specific piece of data out to use in the answer.

Question 11b.

Sample response

Daily smoking leads to toxic chemicals entering the body and bloodstream. This causes sticky blood, which can elevate blood pressure, leading to hypertension. A high percentage of people smoking daily in remote/very remote areas (approximately 26% in 2010) could lead to an increase in burden of disease due to YLD associated with hypertension, compared with people in major cities, who are less likely to smoke daily (14% in 2010), and who therefore have a lower YLD.

Mark allocation: 4 marks

- 1 mark for use of data
- 1 mark for comparison of population groups
- 1 mark for a statement about how tobacco impacts on the body
- 1 mark for a link to health status

Question 12

Sample response

The Victorian Workplace Mental Wellbeing Collaboration is creating a positive and supportive culture. This looks to improve workers' self-esteem, increasing workers' mental health and wellbeing. This can lead to a productive workforce nationally, which can supply necessary goods and services and help the economy to grow.

Mark allocation: 3 marks

- 1 mark for linking to the case study
- 2 marks for explaining mental health and wellbeing as a resource nationally

Unit 3 | Area of Study 2 Promoting health in Australia

Question 1

Sample response

The social model of health, which focuses on prevention, has improved the life expectancy of men and women in recent times (e.g. for women, life expectancy increased from 75 years of age in 1980 to 85 years of age in 2015).

Mark allocation: 2 marks

- 1 mark for outlining a conclusion about the positive impact on life expectancy linked to the social model of health
- 1 mark for using information from the graph; full marks cannot be awarded if information from the graph has not been included

Question 2

Sample response

Culturally appropriate: The Aboriginal and Torres Strait Islander Guide to Healthy Eating is a visual representation of foods Aboriginal and Torres Strait Islander peoples may use to prepare a meal. It represents foods they may consume and provides extra information (on the second page) about foods to avoid and ideas for healthy snacks. Easy to access visual information may encourage a change in diet and assist Aboriginal and Torres Strait Islander peoples to consume more fruit and vegetables to help them meet the recommended intake.

Note: Other possible responses may include varied education/literacy levels are supported due to it being a visual tool.

Mark allocation: 2 marks

- 2 marks for explaining a strength of the Aboriginal and Torres Strait Islander Guide to Healthy Eating, which clearly links back to the dietary habits of Aboriginal and Torres Strait Islander peoples

Question 3

Sample response

The Australian Government uses the Australian Dietary Guidelines and the Australian Guide to Healthy Eating to help change and improve the dietary habits of Australians.

The Australian Dietary Guidelines include five guidelines for overall dietary habits. Guidelines 2 and 3 make some suggestions about nutrient amounts in the daily diet. For example, Guideline 3 suggests limiting intake of foods containing saturated fat, added salt, added sugar and alcohol.

The Australian Guide to Healthy Eating provides a visual representation of the Australian Dietary Guidelines and includes examples of foods and proportions that should be eaten.

While both initiatives provide information to help Australians make healthy choices, they rely heavily on the education and skills of the consumers. For example, if you don't know which foods are high in added salt, how can you limit them? Although the Australian Guide to Healthy Eating has pictures of the foods from the different food groups, it mainly shows individual foods. So where does a pizza fit in? Without some knowledge and skills, this dietary guidance is likely to go unheeded.

Both initiatives also suggest a high intake of fresh fruit and vegetables. This can be heavily dependent on food security and access. Due to geographical location, housing and socioeconomic status, it may not be feasible for people to access sufficient fresh fruit and vegetables, which could inhibit their ability to follow the guidelines.

While both initiatives provide important information in different ways, without further support such as policy change, commercial factors will continue to influence Australians' food selection. The government needs to look at a policy that makes foods that are promoted through the Australian Dietary Guidelines and the Australian Guide to Healthy Eating cheaper to ensure people can access these foods and consume them. Without this support, the capacity for these initiatives to cause significant change in the dietary habits of Australians is minimal.

Mark allocation: 6 marks

This response is marked holistically.

- 6 marks: The response identifies and evaluates two initiatives and their limitations. It also evaluates the capacity of the programs to cause change.
- 4–5 marks: The response identifies and evaluates two initiatives and their limitations.
- 2–3 marks: The response identifies and evaluates two initiatives.
- 1 mark: The response identifies one or two Australian Government initiatives.
- 0 marks: The question is not attempted, or the response is not relevant to the question.

TIP

» **Use specific examples from the initiatives to show a greater depth of understanding.**

Question 4

Sample response

Action area 1: building healthy public policy

This may involve the inclusion of bike paths and recreational infrastructure in the planning and budgeting for remote and very remote areas. This will address the increased number of deaths experienced for very remote and remote communities compared to major cities as it will increase opportunities for physical activity. This will decrease the risk of lifestyle diseases such as cardiovascular disease (CVD) and deaths in very remote and remote areas compared to the lower deaths per 100 000 for people living in major cities.

Action area 2: strengthening community action by supporting the government, local healthcare providers and local community groups to run free health screening and information sessions in very remote and remote areas

This may include the community requesting health professionals to travel to remote and very remote areas to increase access to preventive healthcare. Multiple groups working together for better health will decrease the risk of lifestyle diseases such as CVD and deaths in very remote and remote areas compared to those in major cities, whose residents have regular access to a GP and community initiatives to help provide healthcare information, decreasing the number of deaths.

Mark allocation: 6 marks

- 1 mark for identifying an action area of the Ottawa Charter for Health Promotion (up to 2 marks)
- 2 marks for explaining how the action area could be used to decrease the gap between deaths in different geographic locations; the response must include information from the graph to be awarded full marks (up to 4 marks)

Note: The explanation should show a clear understanding of the action area and a practical application of this to areas outside major cities.

Question 5a.

Sample response

Private health insurance is optional and covers some of the cost of additional healthcare that an individual pays for in addition to Medicare. It can include coverage for services such as physiotherapy.

Mark allocation: 1 mark

- 1 mark for an accurate description (key terms include optional, additional, healthcare coverage)

Question 5b.

Sample response

> The Australian Government wants more people to take out private health insurance as this will decrease the burden on the public health system. They encourage people to do this by offering incentives for taking out private health insurance. One incentive is the Medicare levy surcharge. This is where individuals who earn over a certain threshold (higher income earners) must pay an additional levy (means tested) if they do not have private health insurance.

Note: Other possible incentives that could be discussed are listed below.

- The private health insurance rebate subsidises private health insurance premiums.
- The Lifetime Health Cover loading encourages people to take out hospital insurance by the age of 30 and maintain it.

Mark allocation: 3 marks

- 2 marks for explaining why the Australian Government wants people to take out private health insurance, using one incentive program to support this explanation
- 1 mark for correctly identifying an Australian Government incentive

Question 6a.

Sample response

Smoking: The Quit program has worked hard to phase out tobacco advertising on television and radio. It has made changes to laws in matters such as plain packaging and smoke-free areas. It also runs a quit helpline that offers support and advice for those trying to give up smoking.

OR

Skin cancer: The SunSmart program encourages schools to have policies like 'no hat, no play'. They also advocate for shade when planning new outdoor spaces and they have an app that informs people of the ultraviolet (UV) levels for the day. The SunSmart program has a catchy slogan, 'slip, slop, slap, seek and slide', which encourages people to slip on a shirt, slop on some sunscreen, slap on a hat, seek shade and slide on sunglasses.

OR

Road safety: The Driver Reviver program includes setting up to 220 Driver Reviver sites, which are open each holiday season. These are along popular routes and offer a place to stop and refresh, with free tea, coffee, snacks and toilet facilities. The Driver Reviver program involves State Emergency Service (SES) volunteers, volunteer fire services (e.g. Country Fire Authority) and the Lions Club. The program also offers holiday motoring tips online (e.g. education regarding the dangers of driving when fatigued).

Mark allocation: 3 marks

- 1 mark for describing a characteristic of one program (up to 3 marks)

TIP

» **Use different and specific characteristics of your chosen program to avoid duplicating content.**

Question 6b.

Sample response

Smoking: The Quit program reflects the action area of building healthy public policy. This involves implementing rules and laws with good health in mind, such as increasing the number of smoke-free areas.

It also reflects the action area of creating supportive environments. This is where making the healthy choice is the easy choice, which is also achieved by having more smoke-free areas, and by having a quit helpline for support.

OR

Skin cancer: The SunSmart program reflects the action area of building healthy public policy. This involves implementing rules and laws with good health in mind, such as the development of policies like the 'no hat, no play' policy in schools.

It also reflects the action area of creating supportive environments. This is where making the healthy choice is the easy choice, which is also achieved by ensuring all new outdoor play areas have shade.

OR

Road safety: The Driver Reviver program reflects the action area of strengthening community action. This includes people working together to achieve positive health outcomes, such as SES volunteers, volunteer fire services and the Lions Club.

It also reflects the action area of development of personal skills as it involves education. This is achieved through the holiday motoring tips provided online.

Mark allocation: 4 marks

- 1 mark for showing an understanding of each Ottawa Charter for Health Promotion action area (up to 2 marks)
- 1 mark for explaining how the program reflects each action area (up to 2 marks)

Note: A mark is not awarded for just identifying an action area – more information is required to get one mark.

Question 7a.

Sample response

By subsidising general practitioner visits through Medicare, doctors are more accessible to more people. This may mean that more diseases and illnesses (e.g. cardiovascular disease) are diagnosed and treated earlier, which can increase physical health and wellbeing.

Mark allocation: 2 marks

- 1 mark for showing an understanding of Medicare
- 1 mark for a clear link to physical health and wellbeing

Question 7b.

Sample response

Through subsidising vital medications, the Pharmaceutical Benefits Scheme can help manage more illnesses and diseases (e.g. type 2 diabetes). This could mean people spend less time in poor health, which would decrease morbidity and increase health status.

Mark allocation: 2 marks

- 1 mark for showing an understanding of the Pharmaceutical Benefits Scheme
- 1 mark for a clear link to health status

Question 7c.

Sample response

The National Disability Insurance Scheme (NDIS) provides support and equipment (e.g. modifications to homes) for those with permanent, significant disabilities so that they can live a more independent life. This can increase their resilience and emotional health and wellbeing.

Mark allocation: 2 marks

- 1 mark for showing an understanding of the NDIS
- 1 mark for a clear link to emotional health and wellbeing

Question 8

Sample response

> While it is aimed at workplaces, which may only target some Aboriginal and Torres Strait Islander people, the Yarning it Up – Don't Smoke it Up program has a great capacity to improve Aboriginal and Torres Strait Islander peoples' health and wellbeing.
>
> The program is very accessible, as it is offered to workplaces and communities in a culturally appropriate way. This enables greater understanding by more people, which may result in more Aboriginal and Torres Strait Islander people giving up smoking.
>
> Because the program involves ongoing support, including education and a referral process, it is possible that more Aboriginal and Torres Strait Islander people may give up smoking. This would decrease the number of people smoking now, which could also mean that future generations are less exposed to smoking and that fewer take it up.
>
> By making the information from the Yarning it Up – Don't Smoke it Up program accessible and sustainable, more Aboriginal and Torres Strait Islander people may choose not to smoke, decreasing their risk of respiratory diseases and lung cancer and thus improving their physical health and wellbeing.

Mark allocation: 4 marks

This response is marked holistically.

- 4 marks: The response that evaluates the capacity of the program to improve Indigenous health and wellbeing, with at least two valid reasons that link it to access and sustainability, that clearly link back to Aboriginal and Torres Strait Islander peoples' health and wellbeing.
- 2–3 marks: The response evaluates the capacity of the program to improve Aboriginal and Torres Strait Islander peoples' health and wellbeing, with at least two valid reasons that link it to access or sustainability.
- 1 mark: The response evaluates the capacity of the program to improve Aboriginal and Torres Strait Islander peoples' health and wellbeing.
- 0 marks: The question is not attempted, or the response is not relevant to the question.

TIP

» **To evaluate the capacity of a program, you should consider if it:**
- **is accessible**
- **is sustainable**
- **is equitable**
- **addresses the action areas of the Ottawa Charter for Health Promotion.**

Question 9

Sample response

The 'old' public health model focused on changing the physical environment to improve health: in particular, to decrease the impact of infectious diseases. This included a focus on improving housing. Improved housing led to a decrease in pneumonia and influenza by addressing overcrowding, which decreased the spread of these diseases and therefore the number of deaths. This could account for pneumonia and influenza's decrease in ranking from the fifth leading cause of death in 1968 to the ninth in 2017.

While the 'old' public health model focused on decreasing infectious diseases, the biomedical model of health focuses on the use of technology to diagnose and treat disease. The biomedical model would have contributed significantly to the development of immunisations and treatments in hospitals to prevent deaths. One example is the isolation of a strain of influenza type A in 1935, which may have contributed significantly to the change in ranking of 'certain conditions originating in the perinatal period' from the ninth leading cause of death in 1968 to the forty-second in 2017.

The biomedical model treats individuals once a disease is present. It does not stop people from contracting diseases, especially non-communicable diseases such as cancers and heart disease.

The social model of health focuses on education and the prevention of diseases and conditions. Education has increased participation in harm minimisation practices such as the development of, and adherence to, road rules. This could explain the significant change in ranking for land transport accidents from the fourth leading cause of death in 1968 to the twenty-eighth in 2017. However, as the graph suggests, this model needs to continue its focus on non-communicable diseases to decrease the impact of lifestyle diseases, such as some cancers and heart disease.

All three models have had a significant impact on the number of deaths between 1968 and 2017. Some major causes of death have changed due to the impact of these models, and the models have been developed to reflect these changes.

Mark allocation: 6 marks

This response is marked holistically.

- 5–6 marks: The response includes reference to both sources, shows an in-depth understanding of all three models of health, an understanding of the extent to which each model has contributed to the changes in the causes and number of deaths from 1968 to 2017 and an evaluation of the strengths and weakness of each model.
- 3–4 marks: The response includes reference to both sources, shows an understanding of some of the models of health, shows an understanding of the extent to which each model has contributed to the changes in the causes and number of deaths from 1968 to 2017 and evaluates the strengths and weaknesses of some of the models.
- 1–2 marks: The response includes reference to one source and reference to some models of health.
- 0 marks: The question is not attempted, or the response is not relevant to the question.

TIPS

- It is important that you carefully plan your response before you begin writing to ensure it reads easily and synthesises the information.
- When given multiple sources of information, you should refer to each at least once.

Question 10a.

Sample response

> The Australian Guide to Healthy Eating is a visual representation of the Australian Dietary Guidelines. The Australian Dietary Guidelines were created first and the Australian Guide to Healthy Eating was based on these. The Australian Dietary Guidelines suggest eating a wide variety of foods from the five food groups, so the Australian Guide to Healthy Eating is divided into five parts.

Mark allocation: 2 marks

- 1 mark for showing an understanding that the Australian Guide to Healthy Eating is based on the Australian Dietary Guidelines
- 1 mark for a specific example of how they relate to each other

TIP

- Ensure you know the difference between food selection models, particularly the Australian Guide to Healthy Eating and Nutrition Australia's Healthy Eating Pyramid.

Question 10b.

Sample response

> The Australian Dietary Guidelines, specifically Guideline 3, recommend limiting saturated fat, added sugars and salt. Limiting the intake of these foods can help prevent diet-related diseases such as cardiovascular disease. Cardiovascular disease contributes significantly to Australia's burden of disease through the ill health and morbidity (YLD) experienced by sufferers. Cardiovascular disease also significantly impacts Australia's life expectancy because it can cause premature death (YLL). By adhering to the Australian Dietary Guidelines, particularly Guideline 3, Australia's burden of disease could be decreased, and its health status increased.

Mark allocation: 4 marks

- 1 mark for showing a clear understanding of the chosen food selection model
- 3 marks for a detailed explanation of how the information provided in the food selection model can decrease the impact of a dietary risk on Australia's burden of disease and health status

Question 11

Sample response

> The SunSmart program reflects a social model of health because it seeks to empower individuals to take control of their own health by changing their behaviour. This is seen through the slogan 'slip, slop, slap, seek and slide', which makes suggestions about behaviours. The SunSmart program also aims to educate people about the UV levels of the day through its app so that individuals can be empowered to make informed healthy choices, such as avoiding direct sunlight when the UV levels are high. This will decrease damage to skin cells and reduce the development of mutations that can cause cancer, decreasing mortality rates associated with melanoma.

Mark allocation: 4 marks

- 1 mark for describing a social model of health
- 1 mark for each feature of the program identified and linked to behavioural change (up to 2 marks)
- 1 mark for linking to health status improvements of Australians

TIP

» **It is important to use the information provided in the question, not just pre-learned knowledge about the programs.**

Question 12a.

Sample response

> The PBS, through government funding, has been able to increase the volume of subsidised medication in 2017–18 by 0.8% from the previous financial year to $204.1 million. This can decrease the financial stress of having to use medications to treat or manage conditions, thereby increasing mental health and wellbeing. By increasing access to medications, more people can continue to live a normal life by managing or treating mental and physical medical conditions. This can improve their positive relationships, leading to increased social health and wellbeing.
>
> Increasing access to medications such as blood thinners through the PBS can decrease the severity of cardiovascular disease. This can prevent premature death and increase life expectancy, and can also decrease years lived in ill health (YLD) and burden of disease, thereby increasing the health status of Australians.

Mark allocation: 6 marks

This response is marked holistically.

- 5–6 marks: The response shows an understanding of how the PBS leads to improvements to a specific dimension of health and wellbeing and provides a comprehensive link to health status, and shows a clear understanding of the PBS with relevant information from the stimulus material.
- 3–4 marks: The response shows an understanding of how the PBS leads to improvements in health; there is a link to a dimension of health and wellbeing and/or a link to health status; there is some link to the stimulus material.
- 1–2 marks: The response refers to a dimension of health and wellbeing or health status, but the link to the PBS is weak; there is no link to the stimulus material.
- 0 marks: The response shows no links to the PBS.

Question 12b.

Sample response

> Private health insurance is an optional health insurance that individuals can take out in addition to Medicare. Unlike Medicare, which is funded by the Australian Government through the Medicare levy and Medicare levy surcharge, private health insurance is funded by the individual, who pays a premium.
>
> Medicare only covers basic and essential healthcare. This ensures that essential health needs can be met and allows for resources to be available for future generations. Private health insurance differs because it covers elective surgery and out-of-hospital medical care (extras). These extras add to the cost of the policy, which may lead to decreased sustainability because the cost of cover may not be able to be sustained over future generations.

Mark allocation: 4 marks

- 2 marks for comparing private health insurance and Medicare in relation to sustainability
- 2 marks for comparing private health insurance and Medicare in relation to funding

Question 13

Sample response

Australian Dietary Guideline 3 is titled 'Limit intake of foods containing saturated fat, added salt, added sugars and alcohol'. Decreased consumption of foods containing these substances can lead to a decreased risk of weight gain. This will support Australians to be at a decreased risk of developing obesity and type 2 diabetes, leading to an overall decrease in disability-adjusted life years (DALYs), including number of years of life lost due to premature death (fatal) (YLL) and number of years of life lost due to disability (non-fatal) (YLD). Decreased consumption of foods containing saturated fat can benefit the health status of Australians, as it decreases morbidity caused by the plaque build-up on the artery walls, which can increase blood pressure and lead to cardiovascular disease.

Mark allocation: 3 marks

- 1 mark for correctly identifying Australian Dietary Guideline 3
- 2 marks for outlining how this relates to a health outcome; this can include linking Guideline 3 with burden of disease, health status or a dimension of health and wellbeing

TIP

» **Learn all five Australian Dietary Guidelines and make sure you are able to apply them to initiatives developed in Australia to improve healthy eating.**

Question 14

Sample response

Becoming overweight and obese is a risk factor for many diseases in Australia. It accounts for the second-highest proportion of burden of disease (8.4%) and contributes to cardiovascular disease (19.3%), endocrine disease (44.6%) and kidney and urinary disease (35.6%) (Source 2). Dietary risk is the third-highest contribution of burden of disease and also contributes heavily to cardiovascular and endocrine diseases. These conditions, in addition to impacting on burden of disease, including YLL and YLD, can lead to a decrease in the HALE and an increase in the level of morbidity experienced by Australians.

Nutrition Australia is working to address the impact these diseases have on Australians and support them to consume a healthy diet. The Healthy Eating Advisory Service has attempted to do this through their Pick & Mix 1–6 initiative, providing advice on foods that would be best in a school lunch. Young people who consume a healthy diet are more likely to grow into adults who consume a healthy diet, and would have a lower risk of long-term consequences such as the dietary diseases listed in Source 2. The foods suggested are from five core food groups: fruit, vegetables, dairy, lean meats and grain/cereal foods (Source 3). This information is consistent with other health initiatives that are presently promoted in Australia, such as Nutrition Australia's Healthy Eating Pyramid and the Australian Government's Australian Dietary Guidelines (including the Australian Guide to Healthy Eating), as they base themselves around the five food groups. This supports individuals to make informed decisions, as the various health promotion initiatives are providing consistent messages to Australians about the foods that best support improved health outcomes and can decrease the chances of developing cardiovascular disease and other diet-related diseases.

It can be difficult for Australians to consume a healthy diet as this requires finances to afford a wide range of nutritious foods and time to prepare fresh meals. In addition, people need to have a level of education to understand the health promotion messages and information provided. The Pick & Mix 1–6 initiative has attempted to address this by providing posters to show Australians what food is best to include in lunch boxes, featuring a visual similar to the Healthy Eating Pyramid, which shows the foods that should be consumed the most in the foundation layer and those foods to be consumed least at the top of the pyramid. These initiatives, however, require further funding, as outlined in Source 1. In addition, to support Australians to address the dietary diseases listed in Source 2, Australia needs stronger laws on food advertising to young people and needs to consider adding a 20% health levy to sugary drinks to ensure people are supported to make healthier decisions and consume water. This will hopefully lead to a healthier Australian population and decreased morbidity rates and increased life expectancy due to fewer dietary diseases in the population.

Mark allocation: 10 marks

This response is marked holistically.

- 10 marks: Ideas are organised clearly and coherently. The three sources are used to draw conclusions regarding Australians' ability to improve dietary outcomes and health status. Data/source information is used regularly to justify the effectiveness of the healthy eating initiatives referred to in the source information and link these initiatives to the impact they can have on the health status of Australians. The response demonstrates knowledge of other healthy eating initiatives that complement or work in conjunction with the initiatives from the source material to address healthy eating, and the ability of Australians to make dietary change as a result of these initiatives.
- 8–9 marks: Ideas are organised. Examples from the sources are provided to draw conclusions regarding Australians' ability to improve dietary outcomes and health status. Data/source information is used to support the statements made about the effectiveness of the healthy eating initiatives referred to in the source information and link these initiatives to the impact they can have on the health status of Australians. The response demonstrates knowledge of other healthy eating initiatives. A link is made to the ability of Australians to make dietary changes as a result of the initiatives.
- 6–7 marks: Ideas are generally organised, but may be difficult to understand in parts. Examples from the three sources are provided to demonstrate understanding of Australians' ability to improve dietary outcomes and health status. Data/source information is used at times to describe the effectiveness of the healthy eating initiatives referred to in the source information. A link is made between an initiative and the impact it can have on the health status of Australians. The response may demonstrate knowledge of another healthy eating initiative.
- 4–5 marks: Ideas are generally organised, but may be difficult to understand in parts. Examples from two or three sources are provided to describe Australians' ability to improve dietary outcomes and health status. Data/source information is used but there are limited links to the healthy eating initiatives referred to in the source information. The health status of Australians is explained in general terms.
- 2–3 marks: Ideas are not organised. One or two pieces of source information are listed, with attempts to link these to Australians' ability to improve dietary outcomes and/or health status. The health status of Australians is explained in general terms.
- 1 mark: The response simply restates source information and makes broad statements about healthy eating and health status.
- 0 marks: No suitable response is provided, including incorrect information not related to the concept being assessed.

TIP

» **Questions that are worth more than 6 marks will generally be marked holistically. Consideration is given to the quality of the response, not just whether you have listed some key points for the concept being addressed. You will need to use the source information to analyse the concept being assessed. Generally, in this type of answer you are required to use higher order thinking skills to communicate information in a sophisticated manner. It is important to look for relationships between the source material, as well as similarities and differences between the source material, and consider how these can be used to prove or disprove the concept you are addressing.**

Question 15

Sample response

Measles is a highly contagious disease and could use the benefits of the 'old' public health model, the biomedical model of health and the social model of health. These three models of healthcare delivery have improved health status and could lead to the control and containment of measles in Samoa. The 'old' public health model first used quarantine measures for infectious diseases to ensure they did not continue to spread through the community. This intervention is still used today and would be beneficial to the Samoan people to ensure measles doesn't continue to infect people in the country. In conjunction with other treatment options such as vaccinations, which are part of the biomedical model, which is focused on diagnosis and treatment, this would be effective in addressing the disease and trying to manage its spread in the community to decrease YLD being experienced by the Samoan community. The social model of health uses health promotion messages such as educating individuals about the benefits of vaccinations so they are empowered to make decisions about their health. Furthermore, the social model of health can address the broader determinants of health such as the economic barriers to people accessing healthcare. If Samoa provides vaccinations for free or at a subsidised cost, this will improve overall health status and demonstrate the 'new' public health model.

The 'old' public health model, the biomedical model of health and the social model of health could have worked together to manage and potentially eradicate measles, building on the success and knowledge of the previous model of health.

Mark allocation: 6 marks

This response is marked holistically.

- 6 marks: Ideas are clear and coherent. The response explains how the 'old' public health model, the biomedical model of health and the social model of health are contributing to the treatment of measles. Examples from each model of health to support the response are provided, and the complementary nature of each model of health working towards a common goal of addressing measles is acknowledged.
- 4–5 marks: Ideas are generally organised, but may be difficult to understand in parts. The response describes the 'old' public health model, the biomedical model of health and the social model of health as contributing to the treatment of measles. It provides examples from each model of health.
- 3 marks: Ideas are generally organised, but may be difficult to understand in parts. The response describes examples of the 'old' public health model, the biomedical model of health and the social model of health in general, and does not refer to measles.
- 1–2 marks: Ideas are not organised. One or two models of health are described in general terms.
- 0 marks: No suitable response is provided, including incorrect information not related to the concept being assessed.

Question 16a.

Sample response

> Social justice is about fairness and upholding individuals' human rights. It looks to ensure people have access to essential services regardless of personal traits such as race, religion, age and gender.

Mark allocation: 2 marks

- 1 mark for a statement about social justice (up to 2 marks)

Note: This response requires words relating to fairness or equal rights and removing or addressing discrimination.

Question 16b.

Sample response

> Aboriginal women are under-represented in breast screening due to shame, fear and not feeling culturally safe. The BreastScreen Victoria initiative promotes social justice as it has aimed to increase access to the breast screening procedure, ensuring the basic human right of access to healthcare is upheld for an under-represented group in breast screening. Providing women with a shawl, rather than a standard gown, that recognises their cultural requirements, results in the screening being conducted in a culturally sensitive manner and not just as a standard medical procedure, supporting social justice for Aboriginal women.

Mark allocation: 2 marks

- 1 mark for using information from the case study that demonstrates social justice
- 1 mark for describing how social justice as a concept is evident in this initiative

Question 16c.

Sample response

1. The Aboriginal Breast Screening Shawl Trial allows Aboriginal women to access the program in a culturally safe way by allowing them to wear a shawl during the screening process. This has enabled them to feel more willing to access the healthcare service and screen regularly as advised, ensuring the body and its systems are functioning optimally, improving physical health and wellbeing.

2. A number of organisations worked together to deliver the program; the article stated: 'The Victorian Aboriginal Community Controlled Health Organisation (VACCHO) and the Victorian Aboriginal Health Service (VAHS) led this project and ensured that Aboriginal Community Control was central at every stage.' BreastScreen Victoria also worked with the following partners: Department of Health and Human Services, Deakin University, Cancer Council Victoria, St Vincent's Hospital BreastScreen clinic, Western Health and Women's Health West. This will ensure people feel the program is being delivered by professionals and is trustworthy, decreasing any stress or anxiety associated with the quality of care being provided.

Mark allocation: 4 marks

- 2 marks for explaining how the social model of health is reflected in the program, using a specific example from the Aboriginal Breast Screening Shawl Trial (up to 4 marks)

Note: Students are not required to know specific principles associated with the social model of health, but need to understand the major focuses of the social model of health in addressing the cultural, physical, political and environmental factors that impact on people, improving health.

Question 16d.

Sample response

In the article, it is suggested that the Aboriginal Breast Screening Shawl Trial is already experiencing success as many more Aboriginal women have accessed the service due to trained staff and improved accessibility, and receiving artistic shawls. This program creates supportive environments by ensuring the staff are trained in culturally appropriate practices to allow women to feel safe and included while at the service. The provision of the shawl has made women feel comfortable and has provided them with appropriate modesty during the screen, improving their emotional health and wellbeing.

The mobile screening service being located at local Aboriginal health services means that staff are trained in appropriate processes to screen the women, and helps encourage them to take on this preventative measure rather than requiring treatment for breast cancer later in life. It assists the women in maintaining optimal physical health and wellbeing as it helps them feel confident to have regular checks of their breasts to ensure early detection of breast cancer.

Finally, the partnerships that exist between the range of community services, including VACCHO and VAHS, strengthens the community action. They have addressed the low number of women presenting for breast screens and they have developed inclusive and encouraging ways to get the women involved in their healthcare.

Mark allocation: 6 marks

- 3 marks for an evaluation of the Aboriginal Breast Screening Shawl Trial
- 3 marks for identifying three features of the program OR 3 marks for describing two features and providing significant detail

Question 17a.

Sample response

> Medicare is Australia's universal health insurance scheme. It is provided for all Australian citizens and is funded by the Australian Government through paid taxes.

Mark allocation: 2 marks

- 1 mark for each correct statement made about Medicare (up to 2 marks)

Note: The statement about who is eligible for Medicare must include reference to Australian citizens; a general statement such as 'all Australians' is not acceptable.

Question 17b.

Sample response

> Medicare and the National Disability Insurance Scheme (NDIS) promote access to all Australians by providing for people requiring healthcare or assistance in specific ways to meet their needs. Medicare does this by providing subsidies to essential healthcare such as general practitioner (GP) visits to ensure Australian citizens can access the service regardless of their ability to pay. A GP visit can allow an individual to seek assistance for a condition in a timely manner, therefore reducing morbidity rates associated with the condition and returning the individual to optimal physical health and wellbeing sooner. The NDIS promotes access to better health in Australia by allowing the most vulnerable people with a permanent and significant disability to access healthcare services in a way that suits them through individualised plans, and supports access to other related services such as assistive technology, which will allow people to access their community and be involved in meaningful ways. This will improve their social health and wellbeing as the assistive technology can assist people to communicate and/or independently access their community to engage in social activities.

Mark allocation: 4 marks

- 2 marks for providing an explanation of Medicare promoting health through access
- 2 marks for providing an explanation of NDIS promoting health through access

Unit 4 | Area of Study 1 Global health and human development

Question 1a.

Sample response

Loss of healthy life years (in percentage of total disability-adjusted life year (DALY)) for non-communicable diseases increased (approximately 42%–54%) in the period 1990 to 2010, and decreased (approximately 48%–35%) for communicable diseases, maternal, neonatal and nutritional disorders.

OR

Deaths related to non-communicable diseases (as a percentage of total deaths) increased in the period 2000 to 2011 for upper middle- (e.g. approximately 75%–80%), lower middle- and low-income countries, as well as for the world.

Mark allocation: 1 mark

- 1 mark for a correct trend from either of the graphs

Note: Students must use data to support their answer in order to receive the mark.

TIP

» **Use the graph titles and units when discussing data and trends.**

Question 1b.

Sample response

Similarity: All three brackets (low-, lower middle- and upper middle-income countries) have experienced an increased percentage in deaths related to non-communicable diseases. This means a greater incidence of such diseases and a greater burden of disease.

Difference: Low-income countries have the lowest percentage of deaths related to non-communicable diseases (approximately 38%) compared to lower middle-income and upper middle-income countries. This suggests that communicable diseases still have a significant impact on health status and burden of disease in low-income countries compared to lower middle-income and upper middle-income countries.

Mark allocation: 2 marks

- 1 mark for outlining a similarity
- 1 mark for outlining a difference

Note: Students must show at least one link to health status and one link to burden of disease.

Question 1c.

Sample response

> The global distribution and marketing of tobacco, e-cigarette products and processed foods has increased in the period 1990 to 2011. In all countries, this has increased the numbers of people who smoke, drink and eat foods high in saturated fats, particularly in low-income to middle-income countries. This has meant an increase in the number of people suffering from non-communicable diseases such as lung cancer, liver cancer and obesity.

Note: If the trend identified in **part a.** was a decrease in communicable diseases, students could discuss the improvement of safe water and sanitation as potential factors.

Mark allocation: 2 marks

- 1 mark for outlining a factor that contributes to the trend
- 1 mark for linking the factor to the trend

Question 2

Sample response

Digital technology has enabled many medical advancements and has therefore had some positive impact on global health and wellbeing (e.g. technology allowing earlier detection and treatment of illness and disease). Increased knowledge sharing through digital technology has also assisted in the prevention of many diseases, especially in developing countries. This has led to an increase in global life expectancy.

However, its impact globally is also causing harm, as we see an increase in the incidence and prevalence of lifestyle diseases. These diseases, such as obesity and type 2 diabetes, contribute significantly to the global burden of disease, particularly years lost to disease (YLD). Increased access to digital technology is encouraging a more sedentary lifestyle, increasing the risk of obesity and decreasing physical health and wellbeing. It is also linked to a lack of sleep and increased anxiety, decreasing mental health and wellbeing.

While the initial impact was positive and there will continue to be some beneficial effects on global health and wellbeing, the use of digital technology is causing significant harm and may end up causing more harm than good if we do not change our use of it globally.

Mark allocation: 6 marks

This response is marked holistically.

- 6 marks: The response demonstrates an understanding of digital technology, gives two or three valid arguments to support or refute the statement and shows an understanding of both sides of the argument. A clear link between digital technology and global health and wellbeing is also included.
- 4–5 marks: The response demonstrates an understanding of digital technology and includes a statement about the extent of agreement, includes at least two valid arguments to support or refute the statement, and provides a clear link between digital technology and global health and wellbeing.
- 2–3 marks: The response demonstrates an understanding of digital technology, includes a statement about the extent of agreement, and includes at least one valid argument to support or refute the statement.
- 1 mark: The response demonstrates an understanding of digital technology or includes a statement about the extent of agreement.
- 0 marks: The question is not attempted, or the response is not relevant to the question.

Question 3

Sample response

The Human Development Index (HDI) uses three dimensions and four indicators to measure human development. It measures:

- 'knowledge' through the mean and expected years of schooling
- 'long and healthy life' through life expectancy at birth
- 'a decent standard of living' through gross national income (GNI) per capita.

These measurements provide some insight into the human development of a country. For example, Australia is likely to have high mean and expected years of schooling, contributing to a high HDI of .938, which would suggest a high level of skills and knowledge.

Papua New Guinea is likely to have low GNI per capita, contributing to their low HDI of .543, which may suggest a lower standard of living.

The HDI provides a good indication of a country's human development. However, not all aspects are measured; for example, China has a high level of human development according to the index but people living in the country may not all have the opportunity to lead creative and productive lives, including experiencing gender equity in their country, as these elements of human development are more difficult to measure and don't get considered in the index measurement. Also, as China is a big country, people who live away from major cities may not experience the same level of human development as those who do. This may mean that the index only provides some information about the level of human development being experienced by people of a country.

So, while it can be used to measure and compare countries on some aspects of development, it cannot compare all aspects.

Mark allocation: 6 marks

This response is marked holistically.

- 6 marks: A detailed evaluation (including positives and negatives) of the HDI in measuring and comparing countries' human development, with effective use of data.
- 4–5 marks: A response that demonstrates an understanding of how HDI (including dimensions and indicators) aims to measure human development.
- 2–3 marks: A response that demonstrates an understanding of human development and HDI (including dimensions and indicators).
- 1 mark: A response that demonstrates a very basic understanding of human development or HDI.
- 0 marks: The question is not attempted, or the response is not relevant to the question.

TIP

» **When evaluating positives and negatives, you should refer to strengths and weaknesses and make a judgement.**

Question 4a.

Sample response

Low-income countries generally have poor-quality water and sanitation.

Low-income countries generally have limited access to healthcare.

Note: Other possible answers include low levels of education, low food security, poor quality of housing and high unemployment.

Mark allocation: 2 marks

- 1 mark for each characteristic identified (up to 2 marks)

Question 4b.

Sample response

Having poor quality of water and sanitation can lead to an increased risk of water-borne diseases such as cholera. This can lead to ill health (YLD) but can also lead to increased risk of premature death (YLL) due to dehydration. Increased morbidity and mortality would increase a country's burden of disease.

Mark allocation: 3 marks

- 1 mark for showing that a low-income country is likely to have a higher burden of disease
- 2 marks for a detailed description of how the chosen characteristic would affect a low-income country's burden of disease

TIP

» **When discussing burden of disease, you should show an understanding that this includes both ill health and premature death.**

Question 5

Sample response

Poverty: People in low- and middle-income countries are less likely than those in high-income countries (e.g. Australia) to afford contraception or high-quality education, which can help prevent unprotected sex and reduce the risk of contracting HIV.

Inequality and discrimination: Often in low- and middle-income countries (less so in high-income countries such as Australia), there are cultural traditions that result in decreased rights and less education for women, which can result in unprotected sexual intercourse. This can, in turn, increase the risk of contracting HIV.

Mark allocation: 4 marks

- 1 mark for explaining each factor that links to the prevalence of HIV (up to 2 marks)
- 1 mark for linking the factors to the differences between Australia and low- and middle-income countries (up to 2 marks)

Question 6

Sample response

Increased global marketing of processed foods has a negative impact on health, with it being linked to increased risks of obesity, type 2 diabetes, cardiovascular disease, certain cancers and other non-communicable diseases (Source 3).

Source 1 suggests that low- and middle-income countries have far more disability-adjusted life years (DALYs) as a result of processed food consumption than high-income countries. They experience a greater percentage of global DALYs associated with high blood pressure, high blood glucose, overweight and obesity and high cholesterol than high-income countries.

Middle-income countries are likely to be exposed to increased processed food marketing due to companies expanding into these countries (Source 3) and limited best practice policies in these countries to restrict availability (Source 2). This can lead to increased exposure to foods with high levels of saturated and trans fat, such as pastries, lollies and chips.

Processed foods have a high saturated fat and trans fat content, which means that an individual who consumes these foods is likely to consume more energy than they require. This means that any fat not utilised by the body as an energy source will be stored as adipose tissue, leading to higher body weight and pressure placed on the heart, which will increase the risk of type 2 diabetes and cardiovascular disease. This can put increasing pressure on healthcare systems and lead to a double burden of disease, especially in low-income countries, as they also face problems with communicable and infectious disease, with increased DALYs from conditions such as cholera and dysentery, which can be contracted through unsafe water, poor sanitation and hygiene.

High-income countries also experience DALYs from processed foods, such as overweight and obesity and high blood pressure (Source 1), but with policies in place (Source 2) – for example, government initiatives such as the Australian Dietary Guidelines, greater food security and some countries introducing sugar taxes – DALYs associated with processed food consumption can be prevented.

Global marketing of processed foods has a negative impact on health in all countries, but it is more significant in low- and middle-income countries than in high-income countries.

Mark allocation: 8 marks

This response is marked holistically.

- 7–8 marks: The response includes reference to all sources, and shows an in-depth understanding of the impact the global marketing of processed foods has on health, an understanding of global marketing across all three categories of countries (low-, middle- and high-income) and a clear synthesis of ideas.
- 5–6 marks: The response includes reference to most sources, and shows an understanding of the impact global marketing of processed foods has on health and reference to global marketing across all three categories of countries (low-, middle- and high-income).
- 3–4 marks: The response includes reference to some sources, a statement about the impact global marketing of processed foods has on health, and reference to global marketing in more than one of the three categories of countries (low-, middle- and high-income).
- 1–2 marks: The response includes reference to one source and addresses either a high-, middle- or low-income country.
- 0 marks: The question is not attempted, or the answer supplied is not relevant.

Question 7a.

Sample response

Long and healthy life, knowledge and a decent standard of living

Mark allocation: 3 marks

- 1 mark for each correct dimension (up to 3 marks)

TIP

» You should know the exact wording of all three Human Development Index (HDI) dimensions and the four indicators.

Question 7b.

Sample response

The United Nations

Mark allocation: 1 mark

- 1 mark for the correct answer

Question 7c.

Sample response

I somewhat agree with the above statement. Because Norway is ranked number one on the HDI with a HDI of 0.949, it is likely to have higher life expectancy, mean and expected years of schooling and gross national income (GNI) compared with other countries.

This is likely to mean that, through having higher mean and expected years of schooling than other countries, people in Norway have greater access to knowledge to increase their capabilities for work and living a life according to their needs and interests.

Through having the highest GNI per capita of $67 614, people in Norway are likely to be able to access more healthcare (such as preventive care) than people in other countries as the government will be able to access funds from their people through taxes etc. to fund public healthcare systems and education systems. The high GNI per capita is also likely to allow people in Norway to experience a higher standard of living (through better housing and access to safe water) than people in other countries.

The higher life expectancy in Norway compared with most countries is also likely to reflect that people are able to live a longer, healthier life in Norway than in other countries.

These indicators contribute significantly to a higher level of human development, but the HDI does not measure all aspects of human development.

For example, the HDI does not provide much insight into the freedoms and choices one may have, nor does it reflect participation in the community. These are just as important to human development as the measured components.

So, while there could be a strong correlation between a country's HDI rank and its level of human development (the closer the rank is to one, the higher the level of human development), the HDI does not measure all aspects of human development.

Mark allocation: 5 marks

This response is marked holistically.

- 5 marks: The response shows an in-depth understanding of human development and the HDI's ability to measure this. (This includes its limitations in doing so.) The response clearly indicates the strength of agreement with the statement and clearly links back to the subject of the question: Norway.
- 3–4 marks: The response shows an understanding of human development and the HDI. There is an indication of the strength of agreement with the statement.
- 1–2 marks: The response shows a limited link between human development and the HDI.
- 0 marks: The question is not attempted, or the answer supplied is not relevant.

Question 8

Sample response

> Environmental sustainability relates to the natural environment and using it in a way that will preserve resources for the future. The environment can be a source of natural resources that can be used for trade and/or to provide energy and nourishment (e.g. crops for food) to individuals of a particular country or countries that trade resources with it. Having enough food to feed the world's population would improve physical health and wellbeing as people would be properly nourished and have adequate food security.

Mark allocation: 3 marks

- 1 mark for an explanation of environmental sustainability
- 2 marks for an explanation of the promotion of physical health and wellbeing in a global context

Question 9

Sample response

> Australia has an HDI of 0.938, which is higher than Ethiopia's HDI of 0.47. This is supported by Australia experiencing higher life expectancy at birth (83.3 years), and mean (12.7) and expected (22.1) years of schooling, compared to that of Ethiopia; all these indicators are used to measure HDI.

Mark allocation: 2 marks

- 1 mark for each statement comparing the HDI of Australia and Ethiopia (up to 2 marks)

Note: Data must be used to gain full marks; a response with no data can only gain 1 mark.

TIPS

- » **Whenever a question asks for data, it must be included. Use figures and the correct measurement, such as life expectancy at birth or GNI per capita.**
- » **As this question is a comparison, you must mention both countries.**

Question 10

Sample response

High-income country: a lower level of poverty and higher average incomes

Middle-income country: infrastructure, hospitals and social security systems are being created or expanded but aren't readily available for the entire population

Low-income country: a limited range of industries and high levels of poverty

Mark allocation: 3 marks

- 1 mark for each characteristic provided for high-, middle- and low-income countries (up to 3 marks)

Question 11

Sample response

Climate change results in increased temperatures and extreme natural weather events. Flooding from rising sea levels can lead to crops being destroyed as a food source or people needing to relocate, which can cause anxiety and decrease mental health and wellbeing for individuals. Mass migration can lead to large numbers of people living in areas that are unsuitable for large populations due to limited infrastructure. This allows communicable diseases to spread rapidly as many people live in confined spaces without sanitation facilities or clean water. Disease can be passed on quickly, decreasing physical health and wellbeing.

Mark allocation: 4 marks

- 2 marks for describing an impact of climate change on a dimension of health and wellbeing
- 2 marks for describing an impact of mass migration on a dimension of health and wellbeing

Question 12a.

Sample response

> Social sustainability refers to a society that ensures all people's needs are being met in an equitable way now and into the future. It is about upholding people's human rights so they can participate in society and have equal access to essential resources.

Mark allocation: 2 marks

- 1 mark for a reference to meeting the needs of the current generation and generations into the future
- 1 mark for reference to human rights or equitable access to resources

Question 12b.

Sample response

> Social sustainability requires human rights to be upheld. In a country like Australia, at 0.93 on the Human Rights Index, people would experience the opportunity to access essential resources, which would lead to them being able to lead productive and creative lives in accordance with their needs. In a country such as South Sudan, at 0.17, people would experience a lower ability to access education and healthcare, creating poorer human development outcomes as they may not be able to access a decent standard of living. They would also have limited access to knowledge, limiting their ability to make choices and to meet their aspirations – all elements of human development.

Mark allocation: 3 marks

- 1 mark for the correct use of data
- 2 marks for linking social sustainability to human development

Unit 4 | Area of Study 2 Health and the Sustainable Development Goals

Question 1a.

Sample response

The United Nations

Mark allocation: 1 mark

- 1 mark for the correct answer

Question 1b.

Sample response

The SDGs are important as they can lead to more people globally being able to live in accordance with their needs. The SDGs are attempting to address climate change as it can impact on health outcomes, including safe places to live and reliable food sources. Addressing injustices and inequity will lead to more people being able to access essential resources without fear of discrimination, leading to an end to extreme poverty. This would mean that people can afford essential items such as shelter and healthcare to improve health outcomes.

Mark allocation: 3 marks

- 1 mark for each sentence addressing the objectives to show the importance of the SDGs for human development (up to 3 marks)

Question 1c.

Sample response

SDGs 3 and 12: Achieving SDG 12 is important in achieving SDG 3 because when people are living sustainably and countries are promoting sustainable practices (such as decreasing fossil fuels) more people will experience good health and wellbeing as pollution will be decreased. When we decrease pollution, respiratory diseases could decrease, leading to decreased YLD associated with respiratory diseases such as asthma.

When people in the world, especially in high-income countries, undertake sustainable practices such as reuse, reduce, recycle, they are working towards achieving SDG 12 and this will assist with achieving SDG 3 as resources will be managed effectively and environments will be more stable and healthier, leading to ending the epidemic of NTDs as the climate should be more stable. This will allow more people worldwide to be able to develop skills and capacities in order to achieve a decent standard of living, thereby increasing human development.

SDGs 3 and 4: If we can achieve greater quality of education globally, more people will be aware of important health messages and prevention strategies (e.g. the importance of contraception). This may help decrease the under-five mortality rate (U5MR) and maternal mortality rate globally.

By increasing the quality of education globally, more people may be able to gain a well-paid job. This may assist them in having a decent standard of living, allowing them to lead creative and productive lives in jobs they choose, thereby increasing human development.

Mark allocation: 6 marks

SDGs 3 and 12

- 1 mark for showing an understanding of the relationship between the SDGs (up to 2 marks)
- 1 mark for linking these SDGs to global health (can be dimensions or health status) (up to 2 marks)
- 1 mark for linking these SDGs to global human development (up to 2 marks)

SDGs 3 and 4

- 1 mark for showing an understanding of the relationship between the SDGs (up to 2 marks)
- 1 mark for linking these SDGs to global health (can be dimensions or health status) (up to 2 marks)
- 1 mark for linking these SDGs to global human development (up to 2 marks)

Question 2

Sample response

WaterAid aims to provide safe water and sanitation as well as hygiene education to the world's poorest people.

It addresses SDG 6: Clean water and sanitation.

The purpose of the program is to improve the lives of the poorest and most marginalised people by improving access to safe water, sanitation and hygiene facilities, as poverty cannot be eradicated without these things.

WaterAid relies on partnerships with communities and the local governments to help build clean toilets and provide education to the community.

Mark allocation: 3 marks

- 1 mark for correctly addressing the SDG
- 1 mark for correctly outlining the purpose of the program
- 1 mark for outlining the partnerships involved in the program

TIP

» **You should be able to describe at least one NGO program that addresses the SDGs.**

Question 3a.

Sample response

- decrease maternal mortality rate
- decrease the infant mortality rate and the under-five mortality rate

Mark allocation: 2 marks

- 1 mark for each key feature identified (up to 2 marks).

Note: There are more options that students can use than those two suggested above.

Question 3b.

Sample response

By eradicating extreme poverty everywhere (achieving SDG 1), more people may be able to afford healthcare. This may include contraception for women. By having increased access to contraception, women may have fewer births close together, which will decrease the risk of complications and death as a result of pregnancy, thus decreasing the maternal mortality rate and helping achieve SDG 3.

Mark allocation: 3 marks

- 1 mark for identifying the key features of SDG 1
- 1 mark for identifying the key features of SDG 3
- 1 mark for explaining how SDG 1 can help achieve SDG 3

Question 3c.

Sample response

By decreasing maternal mortality rates, more children will grow up with a mother caring for them. If more people live longer, healthier lives due to reduced deaths from communicable diseases and maternal mortality, increased knowledge can be passed from one generation to another. For example, a mother who lives longer may teach her children about the importance of safe water and nutritious food so that her children can meet their dietary needs and can pass this knowledge on to their own children.

Mark allocation: 3 marks

- 1 mark for providing a relevant example of SDG 3
- 2 marks for explaining sustainability by using examples

Question 4a.

Sample response

> These programs are an example of bilateral aid because they involve two governments – the Papua New Guinea and Australian governments – working together.

Mark allocation: 2 marks

- 1 mark for identifying bilateral aid
- 1 mark for explaining that this involves two governments (Papua New Guinea and Australia) working together

Question 4b.

Sample answer

> Australia provides aid to Papua New Guinea to improve trade (e.g. $6 billion worth of two-way trade in 2017) and improve regional security because Papua New Guinea is very close to Australia.

Mark allocation: 2 marks

- 1 mark for each reason provided (up to 2 marks)

Question 5a.

Sample response

> multilateral aid

Mark allocation: 1 mark

- 1 mark for stating 'multilateral aid'

Question 5b.

Sample response

The program is likely to be somewhat effective as it addresses some features well; for example, it involves partnerships. A number of organisations, such as UNAIDS, World Vision and other NGO organisations, are working together to ensure the program receives the best information and support. This means the reach of the program is wide, and it is more likely to gain attention and the required funding to deliver on its objectives, leading to long-term positive health outcomes for people. The program also empowers people to take control of their lives, while respecting their values and traditions. This is evident as the Fund works with the local people and communities to help deliver the program.

The program is also economically sustainable. It invests in education to improve the skills and knowledge of health workers and communities. This can have positive impacts on employment opportunities, and the knowledge can be passed down through generations, leading to positive outcomes into the future, making it effective.

Mark allocation: 4 marks

This response is marked holistically.

- 4 marks: The response evaluates the effectiveness and demonstrates an understanding of at least two features of an effective program.
- 2–3 marks: The response describes the effectiveness with reference to the features of an effective program.
- 1 mark: The response states the effectiveness with a valid reason.
- 0 marks: The question is not attempted, or the response is not relevant to the question.

Question 5c.

Sample response

The World Health Organization (WHO) priority of 'Power health' includes looking at developing innovative products, services and finance; this would allow the Global Fund to offer safe sex education programs and encourage condom use to prevent HIV being contracted. It would also ensure innovative therapies and medications leads to a decrease in HIV/AIDs, with countries being able to detect illness and provide treatment in a timely manner to return people to good health and wellbeing quickly.

Mark allocation: 2 marks

- 1 mark for demonstrating an understanding of the WHO's priority
- 1 mark for clearly linking this work to decreasing the spread of HIV

Question 5d.

Sample response

Direct social action: volunteering for programs; writing letters to government; joining protests.

Indirect social action: donating money or supplies; encouraging others to donate; participating in an event whereby the entry fee goes towards a charity; raising awareness through social media.

Mark allocation: 2 marks

- 1 mark for each example of social action provided (up to 2 marks)

Note: There are other social actions that students could provide in their response.

Question 6a.

Sample response

1. Promote health: Healthier populations
2. Provide health: Universal health coverage
3. Protect health: health emergencies

Mark allocation: 3 marks

- 1 mark for each World Health Organization (WHO) component (up to 3 marks)

Question 6b.

Sample response

The WHO promotes healthier populations by working towards eradicating high-impact communicable diseases by educating and supporting countries to prevent, control and eliminate diseases such as polio through strategies such as access to medical professionals, and vaccines and other medical technologies. These strategies allow for diseases such as polio to be diagnosed and prevented and announcement such as the one given on World Polio Day possible.

Mark allocation: 3 marks

- 1 mark for identifying an element of the priority of the WHO
- 2 marks for explaining how it specifically addresses the eradication of polio

Note: Other work of the WHO that would be an appropriate answer includes: achieving universal healthcare and addressing health emergencies.

Question 7a.

Sample response

One key feature that is being addressed by Elisa and the midwives is reducing maternal mortality because having skilled attendants present for childbirth in Ethiopia will assist women to deliver safely. Another key feature is ending preventable newborn mortality and deaths of children under five, with skilled nurses to monitor the growth and development of newborns.

Mark allocation: 2 marks

- 1 mark for each key feature provided that is related to childbirth and hospital/midwifery care (up to 2 marks)

Question 7b.i.

Sample response

Sustainable Development Goal (SDG) 5, 'Gender equality'

Mark allocation: 1 mark

- 1 mark for a correct SDG

Note: There is no need for the SDG number, but the correct short title should be used. Students could also use SDG 4, 'Quality education', in their answer.

TIP

» **When questions have multiple parts, make sure you read the subsequent questions to ensure you pick a suitable response that you can use later in the exam to adequately answer the questions.**

Question 7b.ii.

Sample response

SDG 5, 'Gender equality', could assist women and girls, as access to sexual and reproductive health can ensure women are able to achieve optimal health and wellbeing. This will enable them to work and have access to the same opportunities as men, which in turn allows women to be able to afford healthcare options and prevent death from birth or reproductive complications that SDG 3, 'Good health and wellbeing', is looking to address. Gender equality means women are free from violence, which leads to improved mental health and wellbeing, a key feature of SDG 3. If women are able to attend healthcare facilities such as the hospital that Elisa volunteered at, they will be able to seek professional assistance and gain knowledge about how best to take care of themselves and their body when pregnant; this can support women to experience good health and wellbeing.

Access to sexual and reproductive rights, freedom from violence and skilled attendants at healthcare appointments improve health outcomes for individuals. Elisa and the midwives provided extra training for the staff at the hospital in Ethiopia to increase the skilled attendants' knowledge. This can lead to better information being provided to the women attending the hospital, and they can make informed decisions about their healthcare and reproductive rights. Women who have good health and wellbeing can contribute in a meaningful and significant way to their community, enhancing human development. They can be a resource globally as more women experiencing good health and gender equality can contribute to a national economy, which can lead to resources being developed that can be used to engage in trade with other countries. This will contribute to gross national income (GNI) and promote economic progress in other countries. Economic growth can lead to increased infrastructure such as governments being able to provide healthcare and interventions to promote women and their rights globally.

Mark allocation: 6 marks

- 2 marks for identifying connections between SDG 3 and the selected SDG in **part b.i.**
- 2 marks for providing clear links to health and wellbeing
- 2 marks for providing clear links to human development globally

Note: Full marks cannot be awarded if examples from the case study are not present in the answer.

TIP

» **You must know each of the short titles of the SDGs studied in this course: SDG 1, 2, 3, 4, 5, 6 and 12.**

Question 8

Sample response

> Fundraising and using the money to purchase essential equipment for a community, such as to build a water well, can address the communicable disease key feature of SDG 3, 'Good health and wellbeing'.
>
> Lobbying governments and/or decision-makers to address an issue within a community is another type. This might involve lobbying a government to provide a full-time maternal nurse in a regional community to ensure new mothers and babies have access to regular healthcare checks to prevent newborn and child deaths from preventable causes.

Mark allocation: 4 marks

- 2 marks for each description of a social action that can assist in achieving SDG 3 (up to 4 marks)

Question 9

Sample response

> Oxfam Australia could promote health and wellbeing and human development by implementing a number of sanitation systems at a camp where people are displaced. Toilets with bins provide a safe place to dispose of human waste and sanitary products, and hand basins enable people to wash their hands. The people displaced would be able to decrease their risk of cholera, a water-borne disease that is spread when individuals or populations do not have access to toilets to dispose of human waste. This will decrease the YLD and DALYs associated with this disease and improve physical health and wellbeing.
>
> When people have a decreased risk of illness from infectious diseases such as cholera, they are more likely to attend school. At school, they can gain an education, improving their literacy skills; this will help individuals to gain employment and earn an income. An income can ensure people have a chance to make decisions about their life and access essentials such as healthcare, improving their human development and allowing them to contribute to their community in a meaningful way.

Mark allocation: 4 marks

- 2 marks for an explanation of how a non-government organisation operating in Australia could promote health and wellbeing for people displaced by climate change
- 2 marks for an explanation of how a non-government organisation operating in Australia could promote human development for the people displaced by climate change

TIP

» **Learn one or two programs provided by non-government organisations that can be implemented for a range of health and wellbeing and human development concerns; for example, one related to education and one related to clean water and sanitation.**

Question 10

Sample response

> The Australian Government could provide emergency aid if people are experiencing a lack of access to essential services due to conflict. They could provide tents, food and water to relieve suffering; it would be a short-term solution to address the immediate distress.

Mark allocation: 3 marks

- 1 mark for identifying a suitable type of aid
- 2 marks for the description of the aid